The Plainer Truths

of

Teaching, Learning and Literacy

*A comprehensive guide to reading, writing, speaking
and listening Pre-K-12 across the curriculum*

by

Dr. Morton Botel

&

Lara Botel Paparo

OWL PUBLISHING

Owl Publishing, LLC.

150 Parkview Heights Road

Ephrata, Pa 17522

717-925-7511

www.OwlPublishingHouse.com

ISBN: 0-9979065-1-0

ISBN 13: 978-0-9979065-1-6

Library of Congress Control Number:

Cover Design by One L Design, LLC.

Edited by Terri Oppenheimer, Bonnie Botel-Sheppard & Bob Botel-Sheppard

DEDICATION

For Bonnie.
None of this would have been possible without you.

TABLE OF CONTENTS

For more information and resources,
including digital versions of activities, please visit:

www.owlpublishinghouse.com

About the Authors

Dr. Morton Botel

Dr. Morton Botel, Emeritus Professor of Education and Child Development at the University of Pennsylvania, held the William T. Carter Research Chair as Professor of Education and Child Development at the Graduate School of Education, University of Pennsylvania from 1980 until 2006. Botel became the first Reading/English Supervisor and Assistant Superintendent of Curriculum Research for the Bucks County schools in 1951. He authored or contributed to 200 publications and received many honors, including the Lindback Award for distinguished teaching from Penn in 1975. He was selected to write and implement the Pennsylvania State Department of Education Pennsylvania Comprehensive Reading/ Communication Arts Plan to meet the US Office of Education's Right to Read Mandate in 1978 and again in 1988. He expanded professional development opportunities for educators through The Penn Literacy Network, a literacy based professional development program that he founded in 1981 within Penn's Graduate School of Education. Botel was the president of the International Literacy Association 1959 to 1962 (formerly the International Reading Association) and was elected to its Reading Hall of Fame in 1996.

Lara Botel Paparo

Lara Botel Paparo is the Associate Director of the Penn Literacy Network of the Graduate School of Education, University of Pennsylvania. She has instructed teachers in the areas of reading, writing and literacy across the curriculum for 16 years through the Penn Literacy Network. Paparo earned her Bachelor's degree from Franklin and Marshall College in 2004 in Government, and her Masters degree and Pennsylvania teaching certification from the University of Pennsylvania in 2006 in Secondary Education. She taught Social Studies at Penn Manor School District in Pennsylvania from 2006 to 2015.

Acknowledgements and Author's Note

This book has been a true labor of love. It began in 1978 when Dr. Morton Botel wrote the Pennsylvania Comprehensive Reading Plan, and continued to develop and grow into the ideas in this book. This work is different than many in the field of education, and represents both the core frameworks that inform literacy and learning, as well as current research in education. Many of the ideas and texts that are referenced in this book date back to foundational developments in reading, writing, speaking and listening. This provide a solid historical framework for understanding from where these ideas came, and also serves as a springboard for understanding changes in policy, reflecting on how learning can be nurtured in the classroom, and using technology in teaching, learning and literacy.

Dr. Botel passed away while we were re-writing this book, and while he did not get to see the book in its final form, it is his ideas and evolving notions and philosophies about teaching and learning that inform every word.

I would like to extend my deepest thanks to the many people who supported us in writing this book, specifically my mother and father, Dr. Bonnie & Bob Botel-Sheppard for their endless patience and strength in reading and re-reading this text for both content and form, and to Terri Oppenheimer for meticulous copy editing. Thank to the faculty at the Penn Literacy Network for being thoughtful stewards of these ideas, and for their heartfelt support of teachers, coaches and administrators in teaching all students. Thank you also to my amazing husband, Todd, and children, Gianna and Blake, for their support and love through this process.

Lastly, thank you to all of the teachers, administrators, coaches, and community members who contribute to the learning of each individual child.

Lara Botel Paparo

Introduction

As a very young girl I knew that my father was a dynamic and charismatic leader. I wasn't fully aware of what he did for a living but I knew it must be important. He was typically the center of attention at neighborhood and community events and over the years he introduced our family to others in his field who were equally influential individuals—educators, authors, illustrators, and members of the government, for example. As I grew up, I learned to appreciate the enormity of the work that he did and the impact he was having locally, regionally, nationally and internationally. I enjoyed his answer to my question when he came home from a presentation, a meeting or a course that he was teaching: "How did it go today, Dad?" He almost always answered, "This was the best ever."

Those of us who were fortunate enough to be in his circle of family, friends and colleagues gained confidence in ourselves because of his unwavering belief in each of us. It is this spirit and ability to surround himself with exciting and influential people that formed the core of his co-constructionist frameworks: The Five Reading, Writing and Talking Processes, and The Four Lenses of Learning. These frameworks, at their very core, are steeped in the understanding that all people can achieve their very best and live fulfilling and happy lives. He felt very strongly that teachers are partners in helping achieve these goals on behalf of all children.

When I became an adult and my father's student and then colleague at The University of Pennsylvania, I gained a deeper understanding and appreciation of the impact of his work on others. When I was a doctoral student,

I accompanied him to the International Reading Association's (now the International Literacy Association's) annual convention to present with him. He introduced me to one literacy celebrity after another, and after some time I realized that I had just been introduced to more than half of my dissertation's bibliography. It was at that point that I realized how deeply influenced he was by other great thinkers and practitioners.

These stories exemplify the important understandings through which to read this book. This book includes best practices in education—important ideas, engaging strategies and enduring concepts that reflect the influences of important thinkers that span foundational educational research from the 1960's and beyond. This is not typical of many educational books that seek to cite the latest research and the most up to date theories. This work is based upon the foundation of literacy and learning, and is the basis for the strategies and activities that are also included. I applaud this inclusion, as all of us need to look back to look forward, and the core texts of these educational thinkers are infused throughout this important text. A quick search on any search engine would find all types of current research, but one of the underlying concepts in this book is to embrace those who influenced us as we continue to co-construct the best teaching and learning environments --humane, and exciting classrooms that bring out the best in everyone.

Lara's adaptation of, and exploration of the concepts in this book began in 2014, when she and Mort decided to re-write his original text and add more strategies and discussions of digital text and other aspects of learning as they relate to classroom teaching. She and Mort worked together on this until he passed away in July of 2015.

As you read this book, note the key, early influences on Mort's, my own and now Lara's thinking as you look forward to your own co-construction and how these concepts and strategies are enduring and foundational in your classroom and school community.

Dr. Bonnie Botel-Sheppard
Executive Director
The Penn Literacy Network
University of Pennsylvania

Chapter 1
Philosophical Underpinnings

Reform, accountability and best practices: these words have permeated the national dialogue in educational reform over many decades. From the *Right to Read* legislation in the 1970s to *Race to the Top* in 2014 and beyond, the prevailing solution to the problem of low achievement in American schools, backed by federal mandates, has been more testing and more and more test-like teaching. Many districts responded by purchasing scripted, 'teacher-proof' curricula and engaged in initiatives aimed at changing and following the path toward the goals propagated by the testing environment. Over the years, however, research has shown that there has been no significant improvement nationally in our students' achievement on standardized tests, though this improvement has been a goal of every presidential administration. School districts, fearing budget cuts in response to the lack of measurable gains in test scores, have changed curricula, altered teaching goals, and shifted priorities in an attempt to improve student learning in the static way that only test scores can show. Unfortunately, this is not to the benefit of teachers, students, administrators, or district stakeholders, and certainly does not prove educational growth of any individual student or of students as a whole. After spending so many years focused on improving our educational system without any measurable long-term success, it is clear that schools, teachers and students need and deserve something different.

The former Secretary of Education under the Obama administration, Arne Duncan, said in 2013 that our educational system has "stagnated, and that we are lagging behind other advanced countries in academic achievement." According to the Organization for Economic Cooperation and Development, the United States ranks 18th among 36 countries in secondary education, and close to 12% of U.S. students fail to graduate from high school. For inner cities that number is far greater (OECD, 2010). Increased pressure mounting across the country has expanded the use of standardized state tests for evidence of growth, learning and teaching. But while the need for public accountability has demanded that standardized tests prove the outcomes of our schools' efforts, those same tests have proven invalid for designing curriculum and implementing best practices in teaching that produce high test scores.

William Sanders developed the *Tennessee Value-Added Assessment System* to provide a structure to assess school, teacher and student growth over time. Sanders emphasized:

> *TVAAS was conceived as a method of estimating the academic growth of each student over his or her school career in each subject. It does not suggest or prescribe a particular method for encouraging this growth. How you help your students learn is your decision. Typically, students perform on standardized tests whenever good teachers, day after day, promote scholarship and make sound instructional decisions. Teachers measured to be most effective will be those who teach subjects holistically rather than teachers who concentrate on isolated facts and skills that have been tested for in the past. Teaching integrated subject matter is consistent with research on how students learn best and is, therefore, also consistent with good test scores. (2002)*

Thus, high standards for teaching and learning cannot be derived from analysis of individual scores on standardized tests, as they are but a snapshot into a student's learning at that particular time. This perspective on student learning is not the way that data-driven curriculum planning and reform movements have implemented and interpreted Sanders' system, much to the detriment of the best practices that teachers know to be good and effective teaching. Good teaching cannot be derived and contrived simply from the study of test results. Rather, it must be based on valid evidence and theories that enable teachers to develop authentic and productive units in their curriculum across all subject areas. Teachers and students benefit when teachers assume the role of coach, guiding students to engage in critical and creative thinking about ideas across content areas using the processes of reading, writing, and talking.

Similarly, while textbook resources are valuable, they too have serious limits. Powerful states and lobbying groups carry significant influence over the content of textbooks, and textbook company consolidation has given fewer and fewer groups a voice in the textbook writing process. Textbooks should not be the only source of information or the deciding factor when determining the direction of learning. The role of the textbook is to inform, but the teacher should control how that information is conveyed, in what form the learning takes place and what activities surround the textbook. Most importantly, teachers foster an environment rich in resources so that students may see multiple perspectives and hear many voices surrounding topics of study.

Co-constructionism, an idea central to this book, gives a voice to each person engaged in the learning process. Teachers, alone and together, must be supported in co-constructing living lessons based on their own continually expanding knowledge of their disciplines, students, and the evidence-based reading, writing and talking processes. This co-construction spans all areas of learning, and in turn give credence, confidence and authority to each student's participation in his or her own learning.

The purpose of this book is to document the theory, research and practices too often ignored that enable teachers and school leaders at every grade level and across the curriculum to produce higher levels of academic fitness and, consequently, higher levels of achievement on standardized tests.

Defining the problems and finding solutions

Ron Heifetz, in his book *Leadership on the Line, (Harvard Business Press, 2003)* discusses two contrasting approaches of organizational leaders regarding problem solving. He argues that there are two types of problems: *technical problems* and *adaptive challenges*. These problems provide a heuristic model for analyzing where we have been and where we need to be. He says,

> *Leadership would be a safe undertaking if your organization and communities only faced problems for which they already knew the solutions. Every day, people do, in fact, have the necessary know-how and procedures. We call these <u>technical problems</u>. But there are a whole host of problems that are not amenable to authoritative expertise. They cannot be solved from someone on high. These we call <u>adaptive challenges</u> because they require experiments, new discoveries, and adjustments from numerous places in the organization to make the adaptive leap necessary to thrive in the new environment. The sustainability of change depends on having the people with the problem internalize change itself. (p. 20)*

It is clear that too many school systems have tried to solve the problem of low educational performance by thinking of the problem as if it was technical, when really it is a challenge that requires new thoughts, perspectives and change. It is this perspective that has led schools to use standardized tests as the main analytic tool for determining instructional practice.

Through this book, we hope you find a new perspective on the role of experience in each student's educational process. These experiences, named **The Five Reading, Writing and Talking Processes**, are the essential building blocks in planning effective classroom activities, grade level and content-specific curriculum goals, as well as school-wide literacy programs across the curriculum. The goal of these processes is to engage teachers in the development of lessons and classroom environments that foster competent readers, writers, and speakers prepared for life-long learning.

These processes incorporate comprehension, composing, phonemic awareness, phonics, vocabulary, fluency, and integrate these skills in a sophisticated framework involving higher level thinking skills to achieve deeper learning and understanding. They engage students in reasoning logically, thinking critically and creatively, thinking analytically and synthetically, and posing and solving problems — communicating, collaborating, composing and reflecting.

Briefly defined below and comprehensively elaborated in the chapters that follow, the **Five Reading, Writing and Talking Processes** are

1. ***Reading: Transacting with Text*** – *The Process for Listening to, Reading, and Experiencing Texts in All Subjects;*

2. ***Writing: Composing Text*** – *The Writing Process for Composing Oral and Written Texts in All Subjects;*

3. ***Extending Reading and Writing*** – *The Self-Selection Process for Developing Lifetime Reading and Writing in All Subjects;*

4. ***Investigating Language*** – *The Investigative Process for Extending the Mastery of Decoding, Spelling, Vocabulary and Grammar;*

5. ***Learning to Learn*** - *The Reflective and Strategic Process for Reading, Writing, and Talking in All Subjects.*

These processes offer a common language for administrative and teacher collaboration in curriculum development, lesson planning, supervision and assessment. They are not quick fixes, but rather are the core framework of an educational and curricular structure. They must be woven into the fabric of teaching at every grade level and in every subject to enhance students' continuous meaning making, and to enable students to become both independent and interdependent learners across the curriculum.

By the time students leave high school, they should be ready for the life ahead and be reflective, strategic learners who are able to collaborate, question, research, and learn independently. Achieving these objectives will require teachers in every grade, and in every content area, to be as committed to the processes of learning as they are to the content and subject they teach.

In short, accountability as represented by standardized test results is a straightforward technical task. Though it may be easy through these tests to obtain data useful for the assessment **of** learning, it is wholly inappropriate, and indeed harmful, to use these tests to inform and direct the design of curriculum, for teaching, learning, or use in assessment **for** learning.

Chapter 2
The Four Lenses of Learning

The Co-Construction Of Teaching and Learning

Co-constructionism is a fairly recent term for an old and honored ideal; a democratic ideal inspired by our Bill of Rights. It is a call for freedom of speech and the right to hold and advocate for one's own beliefs. It embodies collaborative problem solving, an ideal long embraced by teachers who want to open the minds of students and engage them in meaning making across the curriculum.

Teachers who practice co-constructionism believe that they should support students in keeping an open mind as they transact with all texts. It is important that students comprehend the given facts or literal meaning, but they must also co-construct texts they read by questioning and expanding them and drawing upon their own perspectives in their search for meaning. These perspectives include students' social backgrounds, belief systems and histories, and the thinking and language processes by which they — alone or with others — make investigations and discoveries and come to their own conclusions.

Co-constructionist teachers believe that teachers and students should be engaged in what Schon calls the "chain of reciprocal action and reflection" across the curriculum. This process involves both teachers and students in a respectful dialogue of meaning-making through talking, listening, demonstrating, imitating, questioning, predicting, answering, speculating, interpreting, observing and criticizing. These teachers are committed to the idea that through these dialogic experiences, students will continue to develop as knowledgeable, skillful and unique people as well as productive members of their communities.

Teachers who practice co-constructionism in their classrooms believe that assessment and reporting of students should be, for the most part, performance-based and represented by students' active work; it should include what they say, write, draw, and do. A major cornerstone of a co-constructionist framework is that it balances the products and the processes of learning. While school systems or state mandates systematically dictate and specify curriculum, texts, and content objectives, these mandates too often take for granted the techniques students need in order to master those objectives effectively. Teachers must deal with this reality, but they can also overcome some of these limits by coaching students to learn how to learn effectively and to take increased ownership over the learning process.

This co-construction can be achieved at any age, any level, any content area, and with any set of students Pre-K through 12th grade and beyond. Teachers of very young students are perpetually co-constructing with their students. Observe any teacher of two- and three-year olds and you will encounter true co-construction. The teachers ask questions that stimulate students' minds and bodies and encourage and guide them to make meaning of the world around them. The questions and prompts below can help teachers of any age encourage co-construction in any lesson:

Figure 1: **How to Engage Students in Co-Constructed Learning**

Questions and prompts:

- What does this remind you of?
- What do you think?
- What does this look like?
- Is this different from what we learned yesterday? How?
- Tell me what you know about…
- Tell me what you think about...
- Talk to your classmate about…
- How does this change your mind?
- Why do you think…?

On the surface, many of these prompts are indicative of an inquiry-based classroom. This is intentional, as many aspects of inquiry and co-construction overlap. However, the core objective of co-construction is that the learning is made by and of the students' answers to the questions they pose themselves. The focus on the learning that occurs also provides a structure for the students to then become comfortable with their active role in the learning process.

The Four Lenses of Learning

What makes teaching successful? How do we as teachers determine if our lessons are successful and, if they are not, how do we analyze the learning activities in a way that is indicative of the successes and failures of the experiences in the classroom? The Four Lenses provide a framework for examining classroom activities and environments and a way to both plan and evaluate lessons throughout the teaching process. Learning is not static; it does not stand still for any teacher, lesson, or school, and thus is always changing and shifting as we teach. It is vital that teachers have the tools to evaluate student learning and also to assess their lessons from a variety of perspectives.

The concept of lenses indicates that each of these terms provides a context for evaluating lesson plans and student learning from one particular perspective. They can be used to view teaching and learning from the perspective of each lens in order to further understand the interactions present in the classroom. Teachers can use The Four Lenses to reflect on how each concept is incorporated into the lessons they teach and how they engage with their students in the classroom. The nature of co-constructionist teaching and learning can be separated into **Four Lenses of Learning**:

- Meaning Centered
- Social
- Language Based
- Human

As illustrated in Figure 2, these lenses are not discrete; they overlap and form a vision for learning in the classroom.

<u>Figure 2:</u> The Four Lenses of Learning

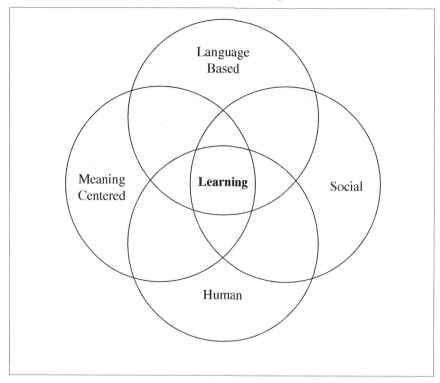

Taken together, The Four Lenses of Learning provide a theoretical background for **The Five Reading, Writing, and Talking Processes** in the chapters that follow. They provide a basis for understanding the complex nature of teaching, and the various elements that contribute to student engagement and learning on a daily basis. In the pages that follow we focus on each of **The Four Lenses of Learning** in order to better understand how and why it matters in teaching, learning, and literacy from Pre-K through high school and beyond, and across the curriculum.

Learning is Meaning-Centered:

People are naturally self-reflective, analytical creatures who instinctively make connections to new information they learn based on the knowledge they already possess, and the experiences they have already encountered in their lives. Describing learning as meaning-centered reminds us that the most fundamental concern of any learner is "making sense." Therefore, in the relationship between the reader and text, the making of meaning is imperative and primary to their understanding of that text. Both reading and writing are co-constructed and transactional activities that designate an ongoing process in which the elements or parts are seen as aspects or phases of a total situation (Dewey and Bentley, 1949; Rosenblatt, 1985). This construct of reading and writing assumes a give and take between the reader and the text. This transactional connection between reading and writing argues that writers construct texts "through transactions with the developing text and the meaning being expressed" (Goodman, 1984). Writers, therefore, create and construct their own texts through the transactions with the texts that they read, bringing their own knowledge, experiences and understandings to the text they write. The Meaning-Centered Lens indicates that the reader transforms the text itself through his or her thought processes as a writer, and through the reader's method of organizing knowledge.

During reading, readers build upon text by transacting with the words and concepts on the page. Through this interaction readers are creating a dialogue with the author. This conversation is completely taking place in the reader's head but it plays a prominent role in his or her understanding and internalization of the concepts read. Although reading is generally considered a receptive language process, this does not mean that the process is essentially passive. Readers use directions from the page to comprehend the author's words but also to question, construct and compose meaning from their own prior knowledge and experiences. In this view, the text does not have simply literal meaning that equals comprehension; rather, most reading must be inferential and interpretive.

Like reading, the process of writing generates and inspires meaning in the author. Students do not simply write down ideas that are fully formed before they are transcribed on paper. The act of composing itself creates ideas and clarified insights. Thus, reading and writing (transacting and composing) are dynamic, meaning-making processes: connections between the text and the reader or writer are developed and changed, discovered and refined during the activities themselves.

Therefore, the learner's prior knowledge plays an important role in reading and writing. For example, if a story is about going to the beach, students who have had the experience of having visited the beach will have an automatic reaction to the reading; they will remember what they previously saw, smelled, felt and tasted when they were at the beach, even if the experience was fleeting. A classmate who has never been to the beach will have no experience to draw from, no personal relationship to the story, and will be less able to draw connections from what he or she has read.

Using language to learn requires actively relating the new knowledge to the known, remembering what is already known or assumed about something in order to relate the new knowledge or information to one's existing structure of knowledge, and making new connections.

There are many types of knowledge important to the acts of reading and writing, including knowledge of the world, of language, of the conventions and structures of texts, and of reading and writing themselves. Since all meaning is made in the context of prior connections and relationships and because each person brings a unique fund of prior knowledge and experience, we should not expect everyone to respond to texts in the same way.

The Meaning-Centered Lens offers a place for student understanding in the reading and learning process. Many activities that activate this lens of learning give validation and credence to student knowledge and underlying assumptions about a particular topic. Brainstorming, knowledge charts and pair-share are examples of activities that teachers can implement in order to activate students' prior knowledge, and also to allow students to begin the co-construction in the lesson that occurs. Through this activation, students can establish or uncover their basic assumptions or understanding about a topic and build upon it through the lesson. The Meaning-Centered Lens is the velcro of learning - without the base, the learning will have nowhere to attach. It must be established so that any new learning has a solid foundation on which to build the new learning that will occur.

As teachers develop or assess lessons according to The Four Lenses, they may also question how the Meaning-Centered Lens is present for each activity.

Questioning Lessons Using the Meaning-Centered Lens

- Did the students recognize the relevance of the activity?
- How was the new learning connected to what the students already knew?
- Did I give the students a target for their learning (the what, why and how)?
- How did the students question or reflect on their learning?
- Have I tapped into the students' prior knowledge?
- How can I help students make sense of the information?
- What will students do individually and/or together to make sense of the information?
- Have I provided the opportunity for students to transact with text (predict, summarize, mark text, draw visual representations, annotate, etc.) while reading or viewing a video?
- How will I relate the new to the known?
- How will I know if/what students have learned?

Learning is Social:

People are naturally social beings. Our need to communicate with one another begins at birth, and transcends language and culture. The development of social constructs in various cultures was born out of these interactions, which remain an incredible reservoir of knowledge and experiences for our students, Pre-K through 12th grade across the curriculum.

Our understanding of how very young children develop competence in oral and written language has grown dramatically over the years. Rather than learning to speak or write by passive imitation of adult models, we now know that children actively build complex repertoires of language strategies in order to make meaning out of their experience of the world (Harste, Woodward and Burke, 1984). Making use of context, children create rules for speaking, and their families, in turn, assume that these early vocalizations are meaningful. Parents and older siblings give feedback to children in some cases by expanding and elaborating on what children say, and in other cases by modeling and telling stories. Thus, children create and recreate language through social activities. Classmates mutually exchange ideas and therefore emphasize communication rather than correcting errors. In this environment, children become increasingly competent language users starting at a very young age.

Studies on early language development indicate the importance of social interaction in learning language and highlight the need for meaningful, interactive language environments to be present in classrooms at all levels. These shared social systems shape cognitive development. When the teacher and learner interact and 'think aloud' about how to do things, they learn how other people think and learn, along with specific content knowledge (Boomer, 1985).

Students acquire knowledge of how to interact, how to communicate with one another appropriately in different situations, and how to make sense of what others say and do in meaningful, interactive environments. Writers assume readers and readers imagine writers. Speakers focus on listeners and listeners attend to talkers. Readers and writers in the real world discuss, plan, research, collaborate, read and edit each other's work. In this interaction, readers and writers can and regularly do come into contact with the social norms and experiences of students from very different backgrounds. In short, students' participation in communities of readers and writers from many cultures can provide the continuing opportunity for teachers to bridge the individual and social aspects of learning.

To learn subject-specific content, students need to learn how to take turns at speaking, how to be effective and appropriate when they get a turn (Mehan, 1979), and how to interact with peers in groups constituted to perform a variety of tasks. As Cook-Grumperz puts it, "literacy learning takes place in a social environment through interactional changes in which what is to be learned is to some extent a joint construction of teacher and student. It is the purpose of an educational setting to make possible this mutual construction" (1986).

Learning is a social experience and the Social Lens of Learning provides a context for establishing a community of learners in the context of the school setting while paying attention to how students learn to use language in social groups. It is not enough for teachers to interact with the vocal few and allow them to drive the class discussion and own most of the responsibility for the communication between students and teachers in the classroom. The Social Lens provides the opportunity for students to relate their prior knowledge to that of others in the classroom; to explain in their own words to a listening ear other than the teacher's and to be faced with opinions different than their own. Activities that include reading aloud to students and providing opportunities for them to work in pairs, triads and small groups greatly increase the amount of oral language students use. In addition, sharing writing within the classroom expands the students' audience beyond the teacher and provides valuable insights and feedback on the social and individual experiences of classmates.

When classrooms function as communities of learners, each student's language processes — including his or her choices about reading, writing and talking — reflect the social and communication networks in the class. When teachers can design lessons that allow learners to use language in authentic ways that are closely related to the functions and uses of language in the wider social world, the students and teacher benefit from the communication that is taking place, helping to further build the common language and processes in the group.

As we discuss reading and writing practices in particular classroom environments, it is vital to pay attention to the multiple layers of social context that inform what is happening. Each aspect of students' lives and the areas in which they interact with others both embodies and reflects attitudes, beliefs, practices and policies about literacy and learning. While teachers may choose (or their curriculum may dictate) the texts for students to read, the same texts may be presented quite differently in different teachers' classrooms.

Collaborative reading and talking about texts, whether written by published authors or by other students, provides the opportunity for students to expand their own repertoire of responses. They can practice listening for similarities and differences within and among texts, and compare an author's reaction to a certain scenario to their own. As students interact socially they become teachers, shaping and elaborating on each other's ideas. Collaboration and groups are critical for language development in schools.

Above all, the community of educators must have the will to change. Teachers and administrators must be willing to set up their classrooms differently, willing to change their ways of planning for learning, and willing to assess whether their students have learned by using their interactions and work. Allowing social interaction in the classroom can be challenging, and must have an underlying structure in order for this to occur in a productive way. Even for seasoned teachers, utilizing the Social Lens can create a daunting lack of control over the learning process. However, the value of the interaction that occurs between students within the context of the classroom is a powerful tool. It can create supportive and important learning environments and experiences that encourage communication and investigation. Activities such as pair/share, cooperative learning (which is different than simply working in groups), and fishbowl activities can both encourage and support the use of the Social Lens within the classroom setting.

As teachers develop or assess lessons according to The Four Lenses, they may also question how the Social Lens is encouraged for each activity.

Questioning Lessons Using the Social Lens

- Did the students have opportunities to interact with one another?
- Did the students share their work?
- Whose voice was heard through the lesson?
- Have I given students the opportunity to share their writing/thoughts aloud, either in pairs, small groups, or both?
- Who will be speaking throughout the course of the period? When? For how long?
- How can I encourage students to dialogue with each other?
- How can the students help each other?

Learning is Language Based:

People learn by using many types of language in a variety of ways. Research emphasizes that based on the language they hear and experience at home, young children organize information that they learn systematically and in a sequence that reflects their psychological and social needs.

- academic vocabulary

The best vehicle for language development is language itself. In order to truly learn and acquire language, children learning their first language and adults learning their second or third learn best when they are immersed in it. Using language does not mean breaking it down and teaching it part by part. The cadence and flow of conversations and the way that words and dialogues occur naturally is instructive and beneficial in language development.

Teaching skills-based lessons like grammar is an aspect of learning language, but it is vital that these skills not be separated from the language itself. Teaching students skills often means presenting parts of language as discrete and separate issues, which removes the language from its context. This makes the lesson and skill harder to comprehend, and reduces the learner's purpose to simply completing an assignment rather than learning what role that skill plays in language and conversations. When we teach surface elements of language separate from their context in language, it is not meaningful, and is not authentic reading or writing but rather a drill, and is unlikely to help students understand how to implement what they've learned in their daily reading and writing (Edlesky and Smith, 1984).

3 Whole language

Information that is taught separately from a meaningful context is abstract, difficult to learn, task-specific and often quickly forgotten. To become skillful readers, students need to be involved in tasks that have real consequences and significance beyond the worksheet itself. Learning language, and using language to learn content, is ultimately personal and unique to each individual learner; students may acquire a shared body of knowledge, but each will learn the specifics of language in quite unique ways.

Language learning is cumulative, and not necessarily linear. It is systematic: it involves the individual learner's experiences, the complex interactions between and among students, and teachers, and the community both in and out of the school setting. Students who are surrounded by rich language environments, purposeful activities, and abundant opportunities for choice use language for authentic and communicative purposes.

The Language Based Lens stresses the importance of the fact that students learn language best by using it purposefully and studying its use while engaged in meaningful communication activities. Teachers often struggle to spend time teaching reading and writing skills when faced with a structured and paced curriculum, or when faced with time constraints that limit the content they can teach. When planning lessons, teachers can try to teach reading strategies and content through content-based text and assignments; this supports students as they learn with and through language processes.

Ideally, curriculum planning is best when based — to a significant degree — on students' needs and interests. While this is not possible in most school settings, adapting lessons based on the needs of the class and individual students to whatever degree possible can help teachers meet students where they are and prepare them to achieve success. This may be in the form of providing students with choices whenever it is feasible. Teachers may give students choices in the books that they read, or in the vocabulary that they choose. Self-selection and determination can be a very powerful tool, and though students cannot experience it every time they are learning, the times that they do can be powerful motivators. Strategies that provide for flexibility and adaptations for students' learning differences empower students of all ability levels to succeed. Both struggling and high-achieving students in this environment have the opportunity to thrive, and teachers are also less likely to feel frustration in the rigidity of the classroom construct.

The goal of the Language Based lens is to integrate and use language in a way that is valuable, contextual, and academic in the classroom. Students use many types of language in their lives. They may have one language that they use to speak to teachers and administrators and another that they use with their friends. The language they use in the classroom is different than the language they encounter on the basketball court, and even more different than the language they use online. Teaching through the language-based lens provides students with opportunities to explore the different languages they use in the many aspects of their lives. It both enables and empowers them to use language for their own purposes and in a variety of ways. It is important that students are provided with academic vocabulary and that expectations are placed on them to use this language appropriately within the classroom.

Creating authentic language-learning environments means integrating reading and writing. Reading is often thought to be a receptive language art while writing is seen as productive, but it is more accurate to understand that they are both constructive compositions. Reading often involves nearly simultaneous acts of writing such as note taking or marking a text. Writers are their own first readers. The processes are reciprocal, and as Smith (1983), Tierney and Pearson (1983) and others have indicated, children need to learn to "read like writers" and "write like readers."

Oral and written language should be continuously related and integrated. As with reading, speakers and writers need to develop a repertoire of approaches; a versatile set of strategies for different tasks, texts and contexts. When presented with the same routines for responding to texts over a period of time, many students never attempt to vary their style of reading to suit different tasks and purposes. Students reading a novel in an English class should have a very different approach than students reading a Biology text, and students reading a Calculus textbook should approach their text in a different manner than students reading the Declaration of Independence in History. Students reading manuals and trade books must employ skills that are even more specialized in order to master their text. Experimentation with a wide variety of types of written text is essential, and teachers who present a variety of approaches to text can better equip his or her students to read, not just in the context of his or her classroom, but through experiences with texts throughout their lives. Language can be very powerful, but only to those who possess the tools to use it for their own purposes. The interactions between the text and the reader and the context for the reading provide opportunities to discuss, enact and present ideas orally for many different audiences and for a variety of purposes. This triangulation between these aspects of learning and the transactional nature of the reader and his or her response to the text is central to the importance of the language itself and the role it plays in the meaning-making between the students and the text (Rosenblatt)

As teachers develop or assess lessons according to The Four Lenses, they may also question how the Language Based Lens is encouraged for each activity.

Questioning Lessons Using the Language Based Lens

- How was language used?
- How was the text selected?
- Were students provided tools for decoding the text in a meaningful way?
- Were reading, writing, and talking interrelated? □□□
- Who did the talking? □

- Who asked the questions?
- Over the course of the class session, when did students read, write, and talk?
- How can I make reading, writing, and talking interrelated, simultaneous acts?
- How can I (or my students) translate the language of the lesson into "student language"?

Learning is Human:

The Human Lens focuses on the intrapersonal dimension of learning and the notion that all learners make meaning in unique ways.

All students bring their own fund of prior knowledge and experience. As they progress through school, students have the potential to develop their own distinctive styles of reading and writing and their own voices and strategies for learning. These styles and strategies are not necessarily internal, fixed traits, but rather what Johnston (1985) calls "states"- features of individual performance, which vary across situations.

For students to develop as increasingly independent learners in a variety of situations, they need to become reflective and acquire metacognitive awareness, or knowledge of their own thinking. As they become more conscious of their own styles of reading and writing and of their own strengths and weaknesses as learners, they become more attuned to different texts and tasks, and more capable of selecting or developing learning strategies appropriate for particular situations.

Attitude has a profound influence on students' images of themselves as readers and writers and as learners in general. Attitudes in this context refer to the beliefs that individuals have about themselves relative to a given task (Paris and Gross, 1983). Students' feelings are powerful components of how they think and learn. This is sometimes referred to as the relationship between "skill" and "will."

There are many variables that come into play when dealing with each student's attitudes and the underlying reasons why a student feels a certain way about his or her learning. The effort each student is willing to spend in completing a school task, and the underlying assumptions students carry about school in general, have much to do with their success in school. The power struggle between whether the student, or teacher, or school system controls the learning can limit or liberate the student's willingness to learn. When the students are in charge of their own learning they are more able and more likely to put forth more effort. When students feel that things are being "done to them" their general feeling of self-worth declines significantly.

Building self-esteem and learning to understand others further depend on exposure to literary and non-fictional texts. These texts present students with significant ideas (McLeod, 1986) and with differences of opinion so that they can learn to dialogue, "doubt" and "believe" (Elbow, 1973), and write on subjects about which they can express deep convictions.

As Freire (1985) explained, reading the word is dependent upon reading the world. Children's growing awareness of the world involves experiences and objects as texts, a kind of reading through experience in which the individual learns and changes. Reading and writing is part of human development; learning to read is an act of knowing - a creative act in which learners come to understand themselves and the social world. Children read the world before they read the word; when they write a new text they not only represent but also transform the world. Looking through the human lens, we see the enormous potential that language has to empower individuals and groups to reflect and act on their worlds.

Feeling safe, successful and worthy are basic requirements that must be present for learning to be effective. Equally important is the way students come to understand and appreciate others. The most effective learners gain energy from positive feelings about themselves and others. However, students who experience failure and who do not see themselves as worthy learners or individuals in the school community certainly do not feel safe. As a consequence, they may not develop self-esteem or the drive to take risks in the classroom. When these issues are not addressed, it can lead to low performance in every aspect of language development and use, as well as diminishing learning in every area of the curriculum.

The intent of this book is to provide a structure and starting place for both inquiry and action; to encourage a process of critical reflection in teachers and school leaders in which theory informs practice and practice informs theory. The goal is to encourage teachers to use it to co-construct its ideas in teaching plans, to apply the ideas in their classrooms, and then to engage in a discourse with colleagues about what they experienced. This give and take with the text, and discussion surrounding the text, is also a reflection of what we ask teachers to try with their classes as well.

A good place to start discussion following teaching is to ask questions such as those suggested in this chapter: How did I encourage meaning making? In what ways was the learning experience social? How did I get students to talk, write and read the text(s) to enhance their comprehension and interpretation of the important ideas? How did I enable students to develop both self-esteem and respect for others?

As teachers develop or assess lessons according to The Four Lenses, they may also question how the Human Lens is encouraged for each activity.

Questioning Lessons Using the Human Lens

- Did every student have an opportunity to be successful?
- Are the students learning to be team players?
- Are all students encouraged and helped to talk and take risks? How does the classroom invite learning?
- What might the students already know about this topic/problem?
- Have I connected the content to the students?
- Have I provided choice?
- How can the students use this in their daily lives?

Using the Lenses as a Tool for Lesson Planning

The Four Lenses of Learning provide a paradigm for learning, and each lens both builds on and supports the other three. They provide a framework for planning lessons in the classroom setting, and also give teachers a context for analyzing lessons. Notably, teachers who use the Four Lenses can determine why classroom activities are successful, or how lessons might be shifted if students are not as actively engaged as the teacher had anticipated. For example, if we deconstruct a basic text-based lesson plan, we can see how the lenses could add to the learning or indicate what is missing.

Sample Lesson and Analysis:

A fourth grade teacher teaches a lesson on the environment using a district-assigned text that all fourth graders read. The teacher asks students to volunteer reading aloud in turn, and stops the readers intermittently to ask text-based questions that can be answered from the content of the text. Following this, all students are given a multiple-choice quiz based on the reading.

How was this lesson Meaning Centered?

The lesson did not ask for or require the students to share their prior experiences with the reading topic. There was no opportunity for the students to share their understanding of the text beyond what the teacher asked or what the quiz assessed. A multiple-choice assessment is a quick and basic snapshot of student comprehension; it is not a gauge for true understanding of a topic or connection between the text and the student. There was no collaborating, speculating or discussion relating to environmental issues based on the students' prior knowledge in advance of, during, or after experiencing the text.

Quick ways to add activities that support the Meaning-Centered Lens:

- The teacher can ask students what they know about the topic — in this case the environment — prior to reading the text to assess students' understanding of the topic. This allows them to make connections between what they know and what they are about to read.

- The teacher can ask students to work in groups and generate questions about the topic.

- The teacher can allow students to write predictions about what they will read after looking at a related photograph or vocabulary list.

- After reading, the teacher can allow students to write about what stood out to them, surprised them, or was interesting to them.

How was this lesson Social?

The extent of the Social Lens was that students heard their peers' voices as they took turns reading aloud. The only voice asking questions was that of the teacher, and the lesson offered very little opportunity for sharing among students.

Quick ways to add activities that support the Social Lens:

- The teacher can allow students to discuss the reading with one another and debate anything implied or controversial within the text.

- The teacher can ask students to turn and talk to one another at various points in the text, asking a question, posing a hypothesis, or asking students to predict what will come next.

- The teacher can allow students to share their written reactions with one another by reading them aloud to one another.

How was this lesson Language Based?

The language aspect of this lesson was rooted directly in the text itself, as the questions that the teacher asked throughout the activity were based solely on the content in the text. The multiple choice quiz that followed offered few variations in the type of questions asked, and did not allow students to create their own versions of the text in their own words, thus expanding their understanding of the content. By limiting their language experience to oral reading and answering test-type questions, the students had no opportunity to use all aspects of language to deepen their experience.

Quick ways to add activities that support the Language Based Lens:

- The teacher can ask students to respond in open-ended questions instead of solely multiple choice.

- Sustained Talking/Sustained Listening: The teacher can ask students to talk nonstop for a short period of time (30 seconds for example) about the topic in pairs. Students talk to their partner and then listen to what their partner says to activate their ideas about the language to use in their writing. Students can then write about the topic.

- Students can interview one another possibly roleplaying from a particular point of view.

How was this lesson Human?

The experience lacked the Human Lens at many levels. The experience was very passive; it did not allow all students to feel successful and did not allow for adaptations for the varied student needs in the classroom. The lesson did not allow for adaptations if the text was too difficult for struggling students. Though the text was approved for fourth graders, not all students in that grade can read at the same level, and reading aloud could cause some students to feel embarrassed by word recognition and/or comprehension problems in front of the class. Students who are assigned a particular paragraph at the beginning of the reading often spend the time before their turn pre-reading their section instead of listening to their peers, and therefore lose the majority of the content in the lesson. Once they complete their assigned section, students might feel that they are "done" and ignore the rest of the reading completely. For advanced students, the lesson was far too simple and did not allow for them to expand on their learning through more thorough questions and adapted activities or responses. These students would likely be bored and distracted. (Please note that this is not a complete condemnation of students reading aloud in the classroom, as it has a notable role and positive impact on the students who experience learning in this way. Rather, it is a discussion about the pros and cons of this type of activity, and suggestions of other ways to reach the same goals with varied activities using collaborative learning experiences.)

Quick ways to add activities that support the Human Lens:

- The teacher can allow students to choose from a variety of questions and question formats (paragraphs, drawings, numerical responses and short answers among others) to show their comprehension.

- The teacher can read aloud to the students or ask for volunteers to read.

This lesson discussion highlights the fact that lessons created in the Before-During-After (BDA) lesson plan format – which we will discuss in the next chapter - can allow for a variety of lesson activities; it can involve each of the lenses and include predicting, elaborating, collaborating, reflecting, writing, and the arts.

Students who struggle to make sense of what they read feel like a failure on a daily basis. These students have difficulty making meaning while participating in school tasks. They may feel alienated from their teachers and peers. They could be ineffective in using language to learn, and possibly even feel hopeless and frustrated at their struggle. On the other hand, students who thrive in school and who are advanced in their learning can feel frustrated and bored as a result of being held to an average reading or comprehension level in their heterogeneous classroom. They have a need that is often minimized or ignored in school.

When testing becomes the focus of schools, students who are high achieving, or even average, command less attention from teachers and administrators. These students, who in many cases have already passed their tests, are marginalized in the classroom as a result of the need and stress of students who have fallen behind. Those students who need support are the squeaky wheels; they get more of the limited attention that teachers can provide given the enormous constraints on the precious little time that teachers can spend with individual students.

It is very important that teachers, administrators, and school boards — as well as state and federal education organizations — work toward implementing evidence-based and long standing best practices in their approaches to teaching, learning and assessment. These approaches should have a goal of overcoming all students' frustration by engaging them in experiences that enhance their ability to learn. The Four Lenses of Learning and The Five Reading, Writing and Talking Processes presented in this book propose ways that teachers can enable students to learn more, to enjoy learning, and to become more productive learners.

Chapter 3
The Before-During-After Framework

Creating effective lesson plans can be challenging for teachers of all grades, pre-K through 12th grade. One of the most difficult aspects of lesson planning is how to construct learning activities that engage all learners. One of the most useful tools of lesson planning, and one that we will continue to use throughout this book as a consistent structure, is the Before-During-After (BDA) lesson plan format. In BDAs, teachers create lessons that are broken into three parts; each designed to help the students actively engage in activities to help them learn.

The BEFORE Activity

The Before section of a lesson is the hook of the lesson. It is designed to activate prior knowledge and set the purpose for the rest of the learning that will take place in the During and After activities. The goal is to access relevant prior knowledge and become acquainted with the text before reading and experiencing it. The Meaning-Centered Lens is prominent in these activities, as the goal of a Before activity is to connect what is *known* about a particular topic or idea to what will be *new* in the lesson that follows for each of the students. These Before activities are often designed to be short, and may be as basic as a review of material learned in a previous class. The Before activity is not simply a hook to interest students in the lesson, but it is also driven by the content of the class and previews an important aspect of the learning that will be a result of the BDA itself.

41

The goals of these Before activities include

- activating prior knowledge,
- setting a purpose for reading that will take place in class,
- discussing new ideas or vocabulary,
- building background knowledge,
- making predictions about what will be read or learned, and
- generating questions individually or among the students in the class
- engaging students with the themes or concepts from the text.

Examples of activities that work well as Before activities include

- creating a KWL or a KWLU chart (see page 46 for an illustration and description),
- brainstorming about a word or topic,
- creating a list of questions about a particular idea or topic,
- viewing a brief video to introduce a new concept, or
- writing about something personal.

The During Activity

The During section of the lesson is where the meat of the learning occurs. This is where students are reading, writing, talking and listening about the concepts and ideas central to the text or main learning goal. These activities are designed to help students read constructively with meaning and engagement, and to use a range of strategies to capture initial responses. The Language Based lens is prominent in these activities, as it is through various reading and writing tasks as students engage with content. These During activities can be individual, small group, or even whole class activities that engage students with and in the learning.

The goals of these During activities include

- engaging with the text and the main concepts of the lesson,
- integrating the lesson with their own prior knowledge, and
- self-monitoring comprehension.

Examples of activities that work well as During activities include

- constructing graphic organizers,
- Guided Lectures (see page 53 for an illustration and description),
- summarizing text, either through direct instruction or in a self-determined summary,
- making predictions and asking questions, and
- answering questions that were previously asked.

The After Activity

These strategies are designed to develop initial responses, to gather data about responses from students, to connect with other texts, to consolidate facts and ideas, and to deepen and extend students' responses. They can be as simple as reading response questions or as complex as a longer essay response. After activities can include class discussions as well as more extensive and structured debates. An After activity can also be as simple as a ticket out the door. The purpose of the After activity — beyond expansion of the new learning from the During activity — is usually to create something that the teacher can use as either formative or summative assessment. Teachers can also re-visit the activities from the Before section of the lesson to make connections, draw upon new information, and ensure that students see their growth through the lesson.

The goals of these After activities include

- reflecting on the content,
- showing comprehension of the text and lesson through a variety of means, and
- extending the students' understanding of the text and/or learning.

Examples of activities that work well as After activities include

- retelling or summarizing the text or learning,
- responding to text through discussion, writing, or drawing,
- evaluating predictions,
- answering questions related to text, and
- creating a visual representation of what they learned.

The BDA lesson plan is a template for creating meaningful learning in the classroom. This structure works in classrooms pre-K through 12th grade and beyond, as it provides an organizing structure for the classroom; teachers can tailor experiences for individual readers, pairs, triads, or other small groups, as well as for activities involving the whole class. It can be used for any type of reading material —literary or informational — and may be used as an alternative to the prescriptive and scripted curriculum.

Many frameworks stress that teachers should plan in units and that the structure of each day is less important in the teaching plan. In fact this is not the case, and certainly not the focus of BDA-formatted lesson plans.

Elementary Applications

In an elementary school setting teachers might use this structure to plan four BDAs to teach throughout the day; one for each lesson that they are teaching to students. These BDAs can be as short as 20 minutes, and serve to separate each lesson into distinctive lessons with specific learning goals and activities. The end of the BDA lesson can be a natural break, either when the students put their materials away and get what they need for the next lesson, or a set break like a special or lunch. Sometimes the lesson takes longer than the time set aside for each BDA, and might extend into the next day or more. A full BDA may not be able to be completed in one class session, but can span multiple days, which is a typical and expected. When a BDA spans multiple class sessions it is important to provide closure to the class and to open the next class day with a brief activity; this maintains the structure of the BDA.

Secondary (Middle/High School) Applications

High school lesson planning can vary greatly based on the structure of the school schedule. There is a huge range among high schools, with some having 45-minute class periods and others ranging to 90-minute blocks, and many variations in between. Each structure presents different needs and opportunities for teachers and the lessons they plan. The importance of the BDA format is even more significant in high school, where students change classes up to nine times a day. The Before activity helps students to separate the last class they left from the new class they enter, and gives students time to focus and think. It can also give the teacher time to take attendance, check homework and complete other administrative tasks at the beginning of class. The After activity provides a second "bookend" to the lesson at the end of class, and is best planned so that students can think about and reflect on the learning from that class before walking out the door to their next teacher. A full BDA may not be able to be completed in one class session, especially when teaching with a class closer to 45 minutes long. Like the elementary section above, some After activities can span multiple days, and that is absolutely to be expected. When a BDA spans multiple class sessions it is important to provide closure to the class and to open the next class day with a brief activity to maintain the structure of the BDA. The After activity can be something as simple as "list the things you still need to do to complete this assignment," or asking, "What are two questions that you still have about _____?" The purpose of these two uses of Before and After activities is to allow students the time that they need to make sense, to promote engagement and active learning, and to ensure that you, as the teacher, have a sense of what they know and still need to know about the topic at hand.

Activities and Lessons that Support The BDA Framework

Example and Explanations of Before Activities

KWL or KWLU Chart: A brainstorming activity that can help teachers to determine what students know about a topic before a lesson. This is an effective Before and After activity.

Steps:

- Teacher asks students what they know (K) or think that they know about a topic, and what questions they have about that topic, or what they want to learn (W).
- Teacher records student responses on the board.
- After the reading, or lesson, the teacher asks students to list what they have learned as a result of the lesson, and records the responses on the board (L).
- The teacher can also help students see if the lesson answered the questions that were generated in the before activity.
- The students then discuss how they can use (U) the information that they learned through the lesson.

Sample Handout for KWLU:

K	W	L	U
What do you know, or think that you know about_____?	What do you want to know about _____?	What have we learned about _____?	How can we use this new knowledge?

<u>Do Now</u>: A short question or statement to which students are asked to respond within a specific time (usually 3-5 minutes). The prompt can be handed out on a worksheet or projected to the class. This activity is designed to engage students in writing. This is also an example of a Collins' Type 1 writing activity. This type of prompt is also a great bell-ringer activity (quick activity that students complete at the beginning of class.) These activities allow students to interact with a new concept, review something they already learned, and pre-write in preparation for a class discussion. A Do Now is an effective Before or After Activity.

Example of a Do Now:

"<u>Please Do Now</u>: Write about a time that you had to learn something new. What did you learn, and how did you learn it? Please write at least 6 lines. You have 3 minutes to write!"

<u>Word Splash:</u> Students write a short story (fiction or non-fiction) using 7-10 vocabulary words from a text. This is an effective Before activity as it helps to activate prior knowledge about key vocabulary and concepts, and promotes imagination and associations between known and new words.

Steps:

- Words are read aloud to students, who copy and then write a short story using all words, in any order.
- Students can work alone or in pairs.
- Correct usage is not graded. Students get credit for completion.
- Students pair share, then volunteers share out their stories.
- The class reads the assigned task.
- In an after activity, compare usage of words. Did students know what they meant? How were their uses of the words similar or different?

<u>Story Impressions</u>: Provides students with the opportunity to predict what is going to happen in a text using 7-10 vocabulary words from the text. This is an effective Before activity as it allows students to activate prior knowledge, promote inquiry and brainstorming, and make connections between the vocabulary words that are selected.

Steps:

- Teacher creates a list of words or phrases that could hint at the text and provides the words to the students (either orally or written).
- Students can work alone or in pairs.
- Students must use words in the exact order given.
- Correct usage is not graded and students get credit for completion.
- Students pair share, then volunteers share out their stories.
- The class reads the assigned task.
- In an after activity, compare the meaning of the text- did students predict the story? How were their predictions similar or different than the text?

<u>Possible Sentences</u>: A vocabulary strategy that activates students' prior knowledge about content area vocabulary and concepts. This is a great Before activity because it sparks students' interest in the text and requires them to predict the text based on the words that the teachers select for the activity.

Steps:

- The teacher selects a short list of vocabulary words from the text (about 10 words).
- The students predict the content of the text by creating a sentence for each vocabulary word or concept.
- The teacher gives students a prompt or question to focus their sentences. Example: "How do bees make honey?"
- After reading, students check to see if the "possible sentences" were correct or need to be re-written based on the content of the reading.

Turn and Talk/Think-Pair-Share: Allows each student to be an active participant in a class discussion. This activity can be an informal way to allow each student to speak and listen, and can be implemented in Before, During or After activities.

Steps:

- The teacher provides something for the students to write or think about, and provides time for each student to write or think individually (this could be a quick Do Now activity or a longer writing assignment).
- Students turn to a partner to share their writing and/or discuss their ideas.
- The teacher can have each group share something that they discussed, share what their partners told them, or what their responses had in common. The teacher can also choose not to have students share their discussions with the rest of the class if there are time constraints, or ask for a few volunteers. Additionally, instead of sharing with the entire class, the pairs can choose to partner with another group more small-group sharing.
- This activity is best done in pairs (not triads or quads) to promote the active engagement of each student.

Written Conversations: This activity allows students to respond to one another's ideas through writing. It is an effective Before or After activity as it allows students to reflect on text and engage the Social Lens while incorporating writing.

Steps:

- Students sit in groups of 4 or 5.
- The teacher provides students with a prompt (on handouts or projected) and each student writes his or her own response on paper.
- The students pass their responses to the person to their left, who reads his/her classmate's response and writes a comment below it.
- The group continues to pass each paper around so that every member can comment on all of the responses from the students in the group.

- When students get back their original papers, they read the comments and discuss the key points on their papers, discussing similarities and differences.
- The group shares 2-3 key points from their conversations to share with the class.

Book Walk: This is an activity that is great for previewing text and determining the text features that students can expect to find while reading. In this activity, students investigate the structures of text and determine the purpose of each feature in the context of the text. This can be done in an investigative small group activity format, or as a whole group with the teacher leading students in the investigation. Some of the important text features that students can investigate include:

- Title
- Pictures

Older students can also investigate text features such as:

- Table of contents
- Index
- Glossary
- Headings or subtitles
- Sidebars
- Pictures and captions
- Diagrams
- Charts and graphs
- Maps

Example and Explanations of During Activities

<u>Double Entry Note-Making:</u> This is an effective way to structure a text for a During reading activity. Whenever possible, teachers can format the texts they give to students in this way so that students are able to read text and make notes as they go. This allows space for questioning, marking and summarizing the text in a structured way. It is also useful to separate the paragraphs with a space to allow for chunking of the text as well.

Example of a Double Entry Note-Making text (using the first few paragraphs from the section in this book from the Meaning Centered Lens):

What The Text Says:	My Questions, Comments and Ideas:
People are naturally self-reflective, analytical creatures who instinctively make connections to new information they learn based on the knowledge they already possess, and the experiences they have already encountered in their lives. Describing learning as meaning-centered reminds us that the most fundamental concern of any learner is "making sense." Therefore, in the relationship between the reader and text, the making of meaning is imperative and primary to their understanding of that text. Both reading and writing are co-constructed and transactional activities that designate an ongoing process in which the elements or parts are seen as aspects or phases of a total situation (Dewey and Bentley, 1949; Rosenblatt, 1985). This construct of reading and writing assumes a give and take between the reader and the text. This transactional connection between reading and writing argues that the writers construct texts "through transactions with the developing text and the meaning being expressed" (Goodman, 1984). Writers, therefore, create and construct their own texts through the transactions with the texts that they read, bringing their own knowledge, experiences and understandings to the text they write. The Meaning-Centered Lens indicates that the readers transform the text itself through their thought process as writers, and through the reader's method of organizing knowledge.	

<u>Chunking</u>: This is when the teacher breaks reading passages, or assignments into "chunks" to foster student learning in manageable pieces. This chunking can help to differentiate for students who have different learning needs, and provide for students to make notes and mark their text in a meaningful way. Teachers can choose to chunk text into even smaller sections than the author, making 1 large paragraph into 2-3 shorter paragraphs. The example that follows is from the section in this book from The Meaning Centered Lens.

Example of Original Text:	Example of Chunked Text:
Learning is a social experience and the Social Lens of Learning provides a context for establishing a community of learners in the context of the school setting while paying attention to how students learn to use language in social groups. It is not enough for teachers to interact with the vocal few and allow them to drive the class discussion and own most of the responsibility for the communication between students and teachers in the classroom. The Social Lens provides the opportunity for students to relate their prior knowledge to that of others in the classroom; to explain in their own words to a listening ear other than the teacher's and to be faced with opinions different than their own. Activities that include reading aloud to students and providing opportunities for them to work in pairs, triads and small groups greatly increase the amount of oral language students use. In addition, sharing writing within the classroom expands the students' audience beyond the teacher and provides valuable insights and feedback on the social and individual experiences of classmates.	Learning is a social experience and the Social Lens of Learning provides a context for establishing a community of learners in the context of the school setting while paying attention to how students learn to use language in social groups. It is not enough for teachers to interact with the vocal few and allow them to drive the class discussion and own most of the responsibility for the communication between students and teachers in the classroom. The Social Lens provides the opportunity for students to relate their prior knowledge to that of others in the classroom; to explain in their own words to a listening ear other than the teacher's and to be faced with opinions different than their own. Activities that include reading aloud to students and providing opportunities for them to work in pairs, triads and small groups greatly increase the amount of oral language students use. In addition, sharing writing within the classroom expands the students' audience beyond the teacher and provides valuable insights and feedback on the social and individual experiences of classmates.

Guided Lecture Procedure: This is a way of structuring a lecture so that students can make meaning with the content and reflect on their learning throughout.

Steps:

- Teachers instruct students to use lined paper and create a double entry notes area to the right of the page (example below.)

- The students take notes from the lecture on the left side, and then summarize, mark their notes, pose questions, and connections to the lecture on the right side of the page.

- Teachers should stop after each 15 minute interval of lecturing for students to have a few minutes to reflect on the lecture thus far, collaborate on their notes with a partner, share questions and connections, and clarify any confusions.

Example of Double Entry Notes page for The Guided Lecture Procedure:

Lecture Notes:	My Questions, Comments and Ideas

<u>Jigsaw:</u> A jigsaw breaks up large text into smaller sections, and allows students to work in small groups to read and understand important aspects of a piece of text or different aspects of a topic using different texts on the same topic. This is a great During activity because it allows students to work together and break down important and critical texts with the support of peers and within a structured assignment. This can also be adapted into an After activity as well.

Steps: (*Please note the number of groups will vary depending on the number of texts teachers select, and the number of students in each group will vary depending on the size of the class.*)

- Divide students into six groups. Each group should consist of four people.

- Appoint one student from each group as the leader and spokesperson for the group.

- Divide the text into four sections (as they make sense) or select four selected texts.

- Assign each group to read one section, making sure students only have direct access to their own segment.

- Students work in groups to answer questions, come to a consensus about their section, and prepare to share their answers with the rest of the class.

- The leader, or spokesperson for each group shares the group's ideas with the class, and all students record what they learn.

Expert Jigsaw: An expert jigsaw is similar to a jigsaw, but has the added piece of accountability for each student and group member. Students take leadership roles by teaching their peers what they have learned after working in groups to determine the central ideas or conclusions about a piece of text.

Steps: *(Please note the number of groups will vary depending on the number of texts teachers select, and the number of students in each group will vary depending on the size of the class.)*

- Divide students into six groups. Each group should consist of four people.

- Appoint one student from each group as the leader and spokesperson for the group.

- Divide the text into four sections (as they make sense) or select four pre-selected texts.

- Assign each group to read one section, making sure students only have direct access to their own segment.

- Students work in groups to answer questions, come to a consensus about their section, and prepare to share their answers with the rest of the class.

- Give students time to read over their segment at least twice and become familiar with it.

- Form "expert groups" by having one student from each jigsaw group join other students assigned to the same segment.

- Give students in these expert groups time to discuss the main points of their segment and to prepare the explanations they will make to their jigsaw group.

- Bring the students back into their jigsaw.

- Ask each student to present her or his assigned section to the group. Encourage others in the group to ask questions for clarification.

- Float from group to group, observing the process. If any group is having trouble (e.g., a member is dominating or disruptive), make an appropriate intervention.

<u>Catch Me If You Can</u>: This activity is a fun game where students try and "catch" the teacher's mistake when reading a repetitive or predictable text.

Steps:

- The teacher reads the text correctly one or two times.
- During the subsequent reading of the text, the teacher replaces some

   of the repetitive words with a different word.
   - o   Ex. "I think I can, I think I can, I think I **can't.**"
- Many of the students will "catch" the teacher and correct him/her.

<u>If I Stop</u>: This activity is a fun game where students try and predict the text as the teacher pauses.

Steps:

- The teacher reads the text correctly one or two times.
- During the subsequent reading of the text, the teacher pauses to allow the students to fill in the word based on their prediction.
   - o   Ex. "I think I can, I think I can, I think I _____."
- The students can chorally predict words to fill in the space.

Example and Explanations of After Activities

<u>I-Search:</u> This is an interactive and student-centered activity that engages students in an inquiry-based research project. Students each select a broad topic, and generate open-ended question that they are interested in exploring, and then gather information to find answers to their inquiry. This is reflective research project is similar to traditional research projects, and can limit the possibility of plagiarism as each student writes to reflects on his or her own learning and inquiry.

Steps:

- Each student poses a question that he or she has about a topic. The topic can be selected by the student after teacher prompting, or within a certain category that the teacher pre-determines for the class. (For example: animals, cities in the world, events from World War One, countries that speak a certain language)

- After they choose a topic, students write lists of questions to help narrow their research.

- Students then conduct research using variety of sources to discover answers to their questions. Students should be encouraged to use many types of sources, including books, primary source documents, databases, websites, academic journals, personal interviews.

- Teachers can ask students to keep track of where they learned information in many ways, depending on the age and abilities of the students. (A KWLU chart would be a helpful tool for organizing their I-search paper)

- Students write their I-Search paper and include paragraphs that describe how and why they chose their topic, a summary of their research process including what sources were used, and where they found the sources they used.

  ** Please note that I-Search papers are designed to be written in the first person and focus on students' inquiry, research processes, and what they learned about the topic. Students can restructure I-Search papers into traditional research papers in middle and high school if the teacher chooses to do so.

Learning Logs: Learning logs can be very helpful in supporting students to reflect on the content of the class, and their strengths and weaknesses as learners. Learning logs can be kept in a separate notebook, or a handout provided by the teacher. These can be very useful in reviewing concepts in preparation for a test or quiz, and also in a student conferences.

Steps:

- Students should be given time in class to complete learning logs, either after a lesson or at a particular time during the week to reflect on the lessons from the week. The logs are similar to journals, and students should write reflectively and in their own words.

- The teacher can collect the learning logs once a month and encourage students to reflect on their learning, as well as any issues that arise through the class.

- Teachers can prompt students with questions to guide students in their writing. For example:

  o What was the most interesting thing that you learned from this text?

  o Explain 5 vocabulary words that you found in the text. How can you remember or use these words?

  o Were parts of the text difficult to understand? What made this text more difficult? What strategies did you use to try and help you?

  o What questions do you still have about this chapter?

  o What part of the text would you like to learn more about? How can you pursue this topic?

Re-Writing/Re-Telling: This is an opportunity to explore point-of-view and bias in textbooks, stories, and primary source documents. Students work either independently or in pairs to re-write a specific text from a different point of view or bias. This strategy can help students to think creatively about point of view and the many ways to perceive events and text.

Reader Response: In this activity, students read a text and pick what they feel is the most important phrase or word from the text and explain why they chose it. This provides students with practice in using the text to support their opinions, and invites them to re-read text for a specific purpose. Teachers can also use this activity to engage students in conversations about authors' choices and word selections, and ask students why they think authors choose specific words and phrases.

Test and Quiz Creation Activity:

Please note that this activity can be used with younger students by adapting the directions, limiting the number of questions that students have to complete and adding or omitting group roles.

Group Members:_____

Create Your Own Test!

In groups of four, create questions that you think could be, or *should* be on our test tomorrow. Each group must create at least **15 questions** and all must have correct answers. For each question that your group creates and that I decide to use on the test, each member of your group will get **1 extra credit point**. There is no limit to the number of questions that you can create of extra credit that you can gain. For example, if you make 50 questions and I decide to use 20 of them, each member of your group will get 20 extra points of the test.

Each member of your group must have a specific role with responsibilities, and all members of the group, regardless of their role, must create test questions.

- **Recorder:** writes all of the questions that your group creates. This person should have neat handwriting and good spelling.

    _____

- **Reporter:** presents the group's questions and answers to the class. This person should have a loud voice and should feel comfortable talking in front of the class.

    _____

- **Researcher**: makes sure that the information in the questions and answers is correct using notes, the text book, or any other source. This person should have good notes, a text book, and should feel like they understand the material on the test.

    _____

- **Enforcer:** makes sure that the group is on task and is completing the assignment and keeps track of time. If the group is not working, this is the person who will be held accountable. This person should feel comfortable telling others in the group to get to work, have a sense of timing, and a thick skin.

    _____

Before, During After Lesson Plan Template

Lesson Title	Teacher	
	Course	
	Unit	

Lenses	Reading, Writing and Talking Processes
☐ Meaning ☐ Social ☐ Language ☐ Human	☐ Transacting w/Text ☐ Composing Text ☐ Extending R & W ☐ Investigating Lang. ☐ Learning to Learn

Strategies

☐ ☐ ☐	☐ ☐ ☐

Objectives	Materials & Resources	Homework
		Due today: Assigned today:

Planned Activities

Before		_____ Minutes
During		_____ Minutes
After		_____ Minutes
Assessment		Reflection

Chapter 4
The Five Reading, Writing,
and Talking Processes

The **Five Reading, Writing, and Talking Processes** are adaptable, co-constructionist best practices of teaching and learning across the curriculum. They are relevant through all grade levels, from Pre-Kindergarten through high school and beyond. While each of the Five Processes is an independent process, they are also interrelated. Each process involves reading, writing, talking, listening and thinking, and fuses teaching, learning and assessment.

The **Five Reading, Writing, and Talking Processes** are outlined as follows:

1. Transacting with Text
2. Composing Text
3. Extending Reading & Writing
4. Investigating Language
5. Learning to Learn

As illustrated in Figure 3, the **Five Reading, Writing, and Talking Processes** are not hierarchical, and have equal roles in students' learning. They are pieces in the learning puzzle.

Figure 3: The Five Reading Writing Talking Processes

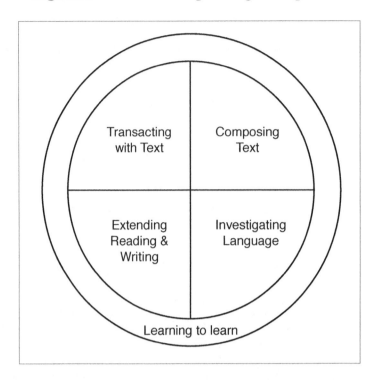

These processes, when taken together, are a model for instructing students as they experience written, oral and experiential texts. Through practice with each process, students become increasingly independent and self-reliant over the span of their educational careers. By their nature and title, these processes are, in fact, processes. They are not subjects to be mastered but experiences that should be regular occurrences within a student's classroom-based education and an individual's lifetime.

While engaged in reading, writing and talking through the Five Processes, students continue to experience and become more proficient in using higher order thinking skills, including reasoning logically, thinking critically and creatively, thinking analytically and synthetically, posing and solving problems, communicating, collaborating and reflecting.

Please note: The evidence supporting each process comes from the meta-analyses of research on oral language development, comprehension, interpretation and vocabulary development, from cross-cultural research, and from the advocacy of the prestigious National Reading Panel and of 22 national professional education associations and the practices of expert teachers and literacy leaders.

Chapter 5
Process 1: Transacting with Texts

Every reading act is an event, or a transaction involving a particular reader and a particular context. Instead of two fixed entities acting on one another, the reader and the text are two aspects of a total dynamic situation. The "meaning" does not reside ready made "in" the text or "in" the reader but happens or comes into being during the transaction between the reader and text.

-Louise Rosenblatt

Transacting with text focuses on the development of active, motivated readers who engage in reading for a variety of authentic purposes both in and out of school. This chapter presents some of the ways all students can engage productively in co-constructive thinking, talking, reading and writing while engaged with literary and informational texts to interpret significant ideas across the curriculum.

The term transacting represents the complex interplay of many factors rather than the simple exercise of skills or passive idea of simply reading. Reading, when comprehension and application are present, is not passive at all. Good readers know this. They practice this in every-day interaction with texts. By referring to reading events as transactions or co-constructions, we emphasize the organic, ongoing nature of the reading process to which readers bring prior knowledge, experience, beliefs and attitudes.

Although knowledge of facts and literal comprehension are clearly basic to making meaning, these are not the hallmarks of true learning, and indeed, they limit the learning to simple memorization. The title of this first process, which emphasizes transacting, highlights the fact that reading comprehension is a complex act and not just a direct translation of the author's meaning or purpose. As Louise Rosenblatt often said, ordinarily there is no single correct meaning of a text. This is true at every grade level and for most texts.

Meaning is not simply 'in the text' to be extracted by readers. Successful encounters with texts are constructive and interpretive; readers of all ages relate the new information to what is already known. They integrate and refine concepts; they make, and not simply take, the meaning of the text. Students learn to read and read to learn—both at the same time. From the beginning, reading is about making sense of the world. In their earliest interactions with text, children bring their knowledge and experiences to the text. A book about an apple can cause young children to think about the apple that they ate with breakfast, or remember a time that they saw someone else eating an apple. The apple is not static; it does not simply reside in the book they are reading.

Similarly, a short story that recounts a young man's experience in school prompts middle or high school students to compare the experiences in the story to what they experience in their school careers — their interactions within school and with their teachers. The experience of the young man in the story is not simply a story. It is a facet of an experience that others can latch onto and from which they can construct meaning that is intrinsic and original to them. Students' reactions to what they read might be different - not right or wrong - based on what they bring to the table.

The word *transacting* is essentially synonymous with *co-constructing*, *interpreting* and *meaning making*, and accounts for their method of comprehension. These words suggest that the meaning of a text resides *both* in the text and in the way the reader experiences and responds to a text. The nature of these responses is clear when students are given opportunities to talk about, write about, and perform their response to a text. It is in that sense that readers' responses can be thought of as new texts - their own texts. Through this construction and reflection, readers are essentially breathing life into their re-creations of texts.

Comprehension is one of the primary goals for students to achieve in relation to a text or idea. Comprehension, in its most basic sense, is when we as teachers can see that a student "gets it," or understands the material or text. However, comprehension has been a limited notion for many. If students are able to simply re-tell a story, it does not indicate that they are able to grasp the meaning of the text, how the story relates to what they already know about the topic, make comparisons and contrasts with their own experiences and determine what they still need to know.

Young children in pre-K through first grade are often thought pre-emergent in their comprehension abilities, but this is a simplistic view of children's abilities at this age, and does not account for children's aptitude in abstract thought. Bloom and Piaget alike have not accounted for these skills. Bloom, in his famous taxonomy, proposed what he called a "hierarchy" of learning levels, beginning with basic knowledge and developing through higher and higher levels of comprehension, application, analysis, synthesis and evaluation. The inference that many draw from this viewpoint is that these are steps to complete; young children should first learn information, then learn to comprehend, then to apply, analyze and evaluate. Webb's Depth of Knowledge, which has joined Bloom in establishing levels of rigor and complex questioning, also introduces the increasing complexities of questioning as levels. Despite the term "level", a student does not need to master one level before moving on to the next. Piaget also identified children in pre-K until first grade as preoperational in his stage theory of cognitive development, which has also led many to assume that they were not ready for higher level, more abstract thinking.

What has become clear from current cognitive theory (and research based on Lev Vygotsky's concept of proximal development and Bruner's concept of scaffolding) is that when learning is guided or supported by teachers, parents, and other students, learners can deal with intellectual tasks beyond their perceived instructional level and ability. Research and observation shows us that young children's co-constructions of texts, as illustrated throughout this chapter, embrace a more complex range of thinking.

We see and experience transacting or co-constructing often — many times without truly realizing or appreciating what we are observing. People who have had what appears to be the same experience will think differently about what they heard, saw, or read, and what it means and how to respond. Consider dialogue and debates of political leaders, or the editorial pages and op-ed pieces in various newspapers, or several reviews of the same book or movie. Clearly these speakers and writers bring their individual styles, philosophies and social perspectives to making their "meanings." Teaching in a way that guides the students among the differing transactions of their peers in their classroom with a singular text engages the entire group in higher-level thinking and discourse.

At the same time, it validates the students in their right to express their own interpretations of what they see, read and experience. Students must come to understand that their interpretations, and those of others, can and should be questioned as well. This process can engage students in conversations of facts vs. opinions, and establishes a classroom that allows for multiple viewpoints on the same text. This is a very important and valuable aspect of the role of the Human Lens in the classroom environment and in the conversation.

Excerpted Reflection of an Early Transacting Experience by Morton Botel on his first granddaughter's (and co-author's) literacy emergence:

Lara's Literacy Emergence

"When Lara, my first grandchild, was less than an hour old, I held her in my arms and read aloud the poem, "Song of the Train." It had great sounds and rhythms like "Clickety clack, wheels on the track, this is the way they begin the attack." When I finished, Lara smiled; everyone present saw that sweet smile. While some doubters would say that a gas bubble caused her smile, our family knew it was her first transaction with literature. For many years before Lara went to school, and for many years after that, Lara heard stories and poems every day and at bedtime.

"Daily reading to our children and encouraging them to transact with these texts is a Botel family tradition. My mother always took great pride in describing to anyone who would listen how she read to me and how delighted she felt in my 'clever' responses. It is also the tradition of many families who understand that this literary experience contributes significantly to the making of a lifetime reader and to the richly informed and literate person. Indeed, practically all children from such literate-rich homes come to school with considerable control over literacy and do well academically no matter how their schools teach. They become adept in literacy because their parents provide them with powerful literary experiences at an early age. Very simply, such parents typically read to their children on a regular basis, tell them stories, talk with them and rejoice in their natural responses and questions.

"What was it that happened to Lara as a consequence of these daily transactions with literature? At first she absorbed the delightful and tongue-tickling patterns of verse: its intonations, rhymes, alliterations and rhythms, as if by osmosis. Later her developing linguistic awareness led her to echo read words and sentences read to her with the intonations she heard. Before long she began to anticipate words in familiar stories and verses, chorally

---

saying them with her parents. Her knowledge base grew as evidenced by her expanding vocabulary and meaning making. She demonstrated this when she talked, raised questions and retold the stories when alone, to herself, her dolls and stuffed animals, and with us. As often as not, she would add dialogue and new thoughts and questions about things not in the story she heard. She began doing pretend reading with her books, first of the familiar stories and then of the unfamiliar ones. She asked questions about her stories and the characters and then about the words such as "Where does it say clickety clack?" Clearly Lara's mind and language were developing and she was becoming literate in ways that children who lacked such experience do not.

"So when did literacy begin for Lara? When was she ready to listen, to observe, to talk, to read and to write? It's clear that it was a process that began in her first days and continued to evolve in ways that we could see and hear and enjoy.

"Two productive concepts are highlighted by Lara's experience: transacting with texts and emergent reading. From the beginning Lara was enabled to co-construct or interpret the poems, stories and informational texts (including books, film, computers and life experiences) in her own way. She was not pressured to learn or master specific things or concepts, yet her vocabulary and interpretation of these texts continued to emerge as she listened, observed, talked and 'pretend' read. She continued to bring her unique prior experience and knowledge into her responses. In evidence was a continuous process of growth and development.

"These concepts have taken the place of or have become more significant than the more traditional concept of reading readiness. Reading readiness has been, and for too many is still defined, as a measure or estimate of the extent to which a child is likely to be successful in formal reading (that is, able to benefit from instruction in the beginning level of a reading series). The problem is that the reading readiness concept is based on a misleading and costly notion. It gives us the impression that reading begins more or less at the age of five or six and is learned essentially by being taught in some sort of sequential way by following the directives of the authors of the adopted reading textbook series. As suggested in telling about Lara's emergence as a literate learner, the learning process is continuous; all of us throughout our lives are engaged in that process."

Not all students entering elementary school have the depth of experience with reading and transacting which is described above. Many students enter school before they are able to read, either because they have limited experiences with reading, because of difficulties with texts or learning, or because they are simply not ready to read. As five- and six-year-olds, this is completely within normal developmental ranges. The reason can be any combination of these, or for other reasons as well. But all students have the ability to make connections, process information, and have opinions and thoughts about the text they are presented.

Larry Sipe, of the University of Pennsylvania, conducted long-term empirical and award-winning research on kindergarten, first, and second-grade students' actual transactions with literature. He was interested in tracking the patterns of children's development of literary understandings as they listened to and responded to children's books. Sipe found that the children's thinking and language in response to literature ranged broadly. Students were able to analyze and interpret the elements of story structure (including characters, plot, setting and themes); connect the text with their memory of other books, authors, movies, artists; connect the story to their own lives; see their own involvement in the story; and respond creatively by changing various aspects of the story, even with limited reading abilities.

Sipe also found that the teachers in his study actively scaffolded this dynamic process with their students by using many of the following strategies:

- reading aloud with the rhythms and intonations of speech, setting a model for the children's reading;

- managing and encouraging the children by calling on all of them and directing their attention to aspects of the story;

- clarifying and probing by showing the children how things related by providing more information, and raising questions; and

- taking advantage of teachable moments where new ideas and vocabulary would be introduced.

The significance of these findings is that facilitating students' transactions with texts at any grade level is a dynamic and spiraling process, not a sequential one. Both students and teachers can be actively engaged in co-constructive inquiry by using many kinds of language to learn. Teachers at the earliest level can and should be active and critical observers and coaches of students' ideas and questions. These can range across the wide spectrum simultaneously from factual learning to higher level critical and creative thinking.

As Sipe concluded from his research, as early as pre-Kindergarten, if given an opportunity, children can demonstrate impressive literary critical abilities. This is drastically different from the view that young children's thinking is pre-emergent. Clearly, the ability of these children's thinking has emerged.

Bringing Readers and Texts Together

The first reading, writing, and talking process focuses on the development of active, motivated readers who engage in reading for a variety of authentic purposes, both in and out of school. Here, reading is viewed as a complex interplay of many factors, not the simple exercise of skills. By naming reading events co-constructions or transactions we emphasize the organic, ongoing nature of the reading processes to which readers bring prior knowledge, experience, beliefs and attitudes. Meaning is not simply in the text to be extracted by readers. Successful encounters with texts are co-constructive and interpretive; readers of all ages relate the new to the known, integrate and refine concepts, and make (not simply take) meaning. Students learn to read and read to learn at the same time. From the beginning then, reading is about making sense of the world. The focus of this reading-writing-talking process is creating a learning environment in school in which meaningful reading transactions or co-constructions occur frequently, throughout the grades and across the curriculum.

Using language in co-constructive and meaningful ways is not new to students who are just beginning their formal education. We know from research that when students enter school, they already come as active processors of language. In their day-to-day interactions with people and their physical environment they have acquired a complex repertoire of strategies for creating meaning out of their experience. When schools introduce reading as a 'meaning-making experience,' the act of reading naturally extends the pre-school child's world, no matter how few or how many specific opportunities a child may have had to engage in literacy-related activities before coming to school.

At every age and grade level, students bring relevant prior experience, knowledge, attitudes and beliefs to reading. When we refer to prior knowledge and experience we mean what they know about the world. This includes what they know about oral and written language and their expectations about the content, structures and conventions of texts they choose or are assigned to read. They also bring information about what is involved in the act of reading itself; what their experience has taught them about reading, and ways to cope with what they do and do not understand.

According to research and theory, our prior knowledge is organized into structures called "schemata." A schema may be a concept or a set of related concepts. Readers use schemata to read between and beyond the lines; what is actually on the page is merely suggestive, never fully explicit. In classrooms, readers need the inclination and the opportunity to access what they already know in order to respond to new information – to relate the new to the known. To help them learn actively from texts, teachers can help students build a context or framework for new ideas, encourage them to extend their structures of prior knowledge, and read texts in light of other texts and life experiences. Lacking a framework, facts or concepts encountered randomly or casually are rarely integrated into the 'known,' and thus quickly forgotten.

Reading co-constructively involves posing questions as well as finding and solving problems. Readers who do this continually ask themselves questions and monitor their own understanding as they work through the text. These readers use a variety of strategies: they plan, predict and keep track of what is partially understood. They hypothesize, search for evidence, and take control of their reading processes. Readers who pose and answer questions while they read build useful, personal structures of knowledge. They are not simply empty vessels or receivers of information. As they read, these readers attempt to integrate new information with prior knowledge. Rather than viewing texts as the authority and reading to find answers to someone else's questions, these students read critically and creatively, taking charge of their own meaning-making processes.

To develop active and engaged readers, instruction needs to be organized so that students are encouraged to become actively engaged with texts, to take a tentative or questioning stance, to go beyond initial or surface understanding, and to become responsible for their own interpretations. Even very young children can be readers who pose questions and solve problems; when being read to by a parent or teacher, young children frequently relate the content to their own experience and expectations. Often, this is because of the ways teachers and parents guide children's co-constructions as they read aloud encouraging discussions and questions.

Active reading also involves readers' knowledge of their own reading processes and strategies — their 'metacognition'. Effective readers are at least tangentially aware of (a) what they bring to the text — prior knowledge, belief systems, attitudes, experiences; (b) what the text brings to them including features of structure, content, form, illustrations; and (c) what purposes and expectations are implied in the reading task, as defined by the reader or the teacher. Strategies or processes are in turn governed by the *purpose* of the reading activity and the kind of text involved in it. Depending on the type of text, students can choose to preview the text or not. They can read quickly or slowly, mark the text or read in a relaxed way. Reading with purpose helps readers keep track of what they read and experience so that when the text presents difficulties they can use some further strategy to comprehend. In purposeful reading, the learner cares enough about the text to use these strategies for understanding what is not immediately understood. When reading in school is regarded simply as 'completing assignments' and students are not invested or engaged in the transaction, students will have much more difficulty learning to read strategically.

For students to develop as active and strategic readers, schools need to provide access to a wide range of texts at every grade level and in every subject. By texts this means not only textbooks but also all types of printed and digital texts — from stories, poems or novels to textbooks, monographs, journal articles and newspapers. It should include materials authored by students themselves about their own life experiences. Texts can also be experiential and include lectures, science labs and experiments, field trips, and other learning activities. School librarians and media specialists are essential, as they are able to help teachers develop flexible and movable collections of books (including books with reading levels at, below and above grade level), periodicals, videos, databases and computer- and web-based programs and apps that correlate with units of study in every content area. They can also help students locate appropriate materials themselves and engage readers with varied and related topics to expand and extend student engagement in the reading and transaction process.

Genres of Texts

Texts read in school can be grouped into two general categories: **literary** (including fiction, drama and poetry) and **informational** (including any other type of writing designed primarily to inform or persuade). Although there are many common aspects of transacting with text that do not change between literary and informational texts, each also has a specific role and unique qualities that support the transaction between the reader and each type of text itself. Beyond literary and informational texts there are also sub-genres of text that students experience in school. Each of these falls into the category of either informational or literary, but has additional specifications that are unique and helpful in supportive as students navigate texts.

Literary Texts

Beginning in early childhood classrooms and extending through the primary grades and beyond, literature plays a key role in becoming a reader. Reading and responding to literature expands the lives of students by broadening and enriching their experience. It enhances their pleasure and appreciation of language when used as a medium of art and acquaints them with the literary traditions of various periods and cultures. Literature offers many opportunities for talking, listening, reading, writing, and using the arts, including interactions that are based on the students' own literary writing.

To provide these opportunities, students need to be aesthetically engaged with a wide variety of literary genres. Anthologies and compilations of short stories is simply not enough.

In order for students to learn the varied ways that they can interact with text and language, they need to read many types of books, with many different topics and styles. They need to be able to "live through" (Rosenblatt, 1961) many different reading experiences and discover what they like and dislike as well as learn their strengths and weaknesses in reading as they connect to large variations in style and material. Experiencing literary text involves paying close attention to ideas, feelings, images, situations and characters. Reading and responding also involve the exploration of universal themes and the realities of one's own life in relation to what the literature says or shows about significant social, ethical, aesthetic, cultural and political concepts.

With literary texts, the goal is not to answer a set of questions or to arrive at a single meaning or interpretation. The text is not the only source of meaning; readers bring their own histories. Reading literature means co-constructing meaning with the author, with the teacher, and with classmates.

Informational Texts

Much of the reading that people experience in their lives is nonfiction or informational text. This means that it is critical for students of all grade levels to spend significant time reading and learning to read nonfiction. A national study sponsored by the Kaiser Family Foundation in 2010 found that students chose to spend less than four minutes per day reading informational text at home (Rideout, Foehr, & Roberts, 2010). Even more troubling, in low income schools, first-grade students can spend as little as 2 minutes reading non-fiction text. (Duke 2000). The importance of these texts and the role that they play cannot be overstated. These informational texts come in many formats, including digital text, online text and app-based text.

It is not just enough to place a textbook in front of a student and call it a day. In addition to textbooks, students need to encounter an increasing variety of informational and expository materials including not just textbooks, but also manuals, trade books, essays, newspapers, blogs, magazines, journals, digital text, primary source documents, and experience itself. These informational texts can inform, persuade, or do both.

Textbooks are a quick and easy resource, and for many teachers they are the only resource provided by the district. Increasingly however, textbook companies have consolidated significantly so that only three major textbook companies control the majority of the textbook market in the United States. This narrowing of the field also causes a narrowing of ideas, and a reduction in the number of voices and perspectives that are presented as the textbook truth. Bias, perspective, and even the choice of whose story is written in the textbook limits the voice of the "truth". Because of the inherent reliability of the idea of a textbook (not to be confused with the reliability of the textbook itself), students tend not to question its content because they view textbooks themselves as the keepers of the truths. Because this is not always the case, students in all levels — but especially in middle and high school classrooms — need to question the validity of what they read. In our increasingly digital world, the range of truth that accompanies text that *looks* valid increases at a staggering rate. Students can be easily swayed by resources that claim to have factual information and must have the tools they need to question the text and validate what they read.

Similar to textbooks, websites that look reliable and as if they contain true information can often be regarded as factual when they are actually not reliable. Therefore, it has become even more important to stress that students question the informational text they read and to question it in relation to other texts of that they know to be reliable sources of good information. These reliable texts and resources should first come from their teachers or libraries, and eventually students can navigate through these resources on their own. Much of the time, questioning the validity of texts takes a lot of teacher modeling and scaffolding until students become more knowledgeable about the process and comfortable with evaluating what they find.

When students are able to access primary source documents, they must cope with material written for audiences other than themselves. The text is different, and concepts and language structure can be very different than their own vernacular. They must make sense of it by relating to the text in a different way, and that relation is often difficult for students to achieve, particularly because they lack reading structures and strategies to help them analyze text in context. When reading these primary source documents, students can be encouraged to think contextually. For example, they can consider how historians write about history, the kinds of documents they use and how they select and manage historical evidence. Persuasive materials invite critical and creative thinking and reading, and lend themselves to debate and the development of arguments.

Students in the primary grades Pre-K through third grade also need informational text presented and taught in their classrooms. These young students benefit when they are presented with early reading strategies that help them understand the concepts as well as the structure of the text they encounter. These strategies greatly assist them with comprehension, and continue to scaffold students as they make their way through their elementary classes.

In the middle and upper grades, part of the difficulty that students encounter in writing may be explained by their limited exposure as readers to materials that take a position and argue for it. When possible, students can benefit from seeing whole texts written for authentic purposes in the world and brought into the classroom. These whole texts often make better reading materials than fragments, as students get to see the context of the information they are learning. These types of authentic, real world texts are always superior to materials written or rewritten strictly for school use.

Poetry

Though many believe it to be literary in nature, poetry really is its own genre of text, with categories further separating the genre by style. Each type of poem, whether a sonnet, free verse or haiku, is experienced differently by the reader. As with the literary and informational texts described above, poetry is most effective when presented within the context of co-construction, and when students are allowed to transact with the literary features, symbolism, and prose of the poem. Children of all grade levels should be exposed to poetry and rhyming (though the two are not always interchangeable) and allowed to make sense of it based on their own prior knowledge before being presented with the "correct" interpretation of the meaning in the text. Indeed, as we discuss writing and constructing text, students should have many opportunities to interact with different types of poetry and make the meaning as they construct their own texts as well.

At all levels, reading poetry aloud highlights the lyrical prose and presents the readers with variations in tone and emphasis. Students can pantomime as a classmate reads aloud, or a group can pantomime in chorus. Pantomime brings all students into the activity, makes poetry fun, and results in a co-construction of poetry on many levels, bringing intellectual, emotional and physical learning into play.

With students in the middle grades and above, a text rendering of a poem can be very interesting and productive as it allows students to see what stands out to their peers; it further emphasizes the point that there may be no correct or incorrect way to make meaning or derive meaning from a poem. To do a text rendering, students use any text (in this case poetry) and either read independently or listen to the teacher read aloud. After reading the text, students are invited to interpret the text by reading aloud the line or verse that stands out to them. They can comment on either the intonation or the meaning of each line or verse in the poem, either as a class or in pairs. Poetry can also be used as a Before activity in a content area classroom if the poem connects with the topic, theme, or particular aspect of the lesson and learning activity.

Consider the first stanza of Sy Kahn's "Boy with Frogs":

> Under his relentless eye,
>
> Jarred and jeered,
>
> The small frogs hop
>
> And pulse in their
>
> Suddenly glass world

From this rich text many questions are likely to come to mind. Whose relentless eye? What does the choice of the word relentless add to the poem? Suppose the poet had used staring instead. Would this word be as effective? What are the meanings of jarred? Can two different meanings of jarred apply at the same time? Who, or what, is jarred and jeered? What do you visualize when you hear the word pulse? What is a glass world? Why is it a suddenly glass world?

These interpretive questions lead students deeper into the poem. Semantic development takes place naturally as students deal with new words in the context of literature. Of course, the questions and vocabulary should be discussed only after the poem has been listened to and read chorally one or more times.

This poem readily calls up personal associations in readers. This poem can lend itself to many contexts and discussions — about nature, cruelty, environment and science, as well as many others. Asking students to deal with their responses to literature adds to their own understanding, and the understanding of others.

Historical and Legal Texts

Historical texts include primary source documents, analysis of historical events, and portrayals of history through different perspectives. This type of text is complex and difficult for students in the elementary grades to navigate; it continues to be a challenge for students through high school and beyond. Students who transact with this text need to understand the words on the page and also see the context of the text as it pertains to a particular time period. Language and vocabulary choices are hard to maneuver, and students who do not have any knowledge of a particular era will certainly struggle to contextualize the importance of one perspective over another.

Students benefit from the BDA format the most when it can provide that context, and surround the text with pieces that help develop a thorough understanding of the time period, other perspectives, and the understanding of the importance of such a document or event.

Much of the transacting that students can do with these content-specific texts is in the validating or invalidating of particular perspectives from the time period, whether it is reading and reacting to a letter from a soldier in the U.S. Civil War or analyzing the opinion of a Supreme Court case. With historical textbooks it is also important to provide students with the tools necessary to decode and interpret them. Much of historical textbook space is dedicated to charts, graphs, images and graphics, and students need to have the ability to decode these as well as the content-specific text that they encounter in this genre.

Historical text needs to be understood within the greater context, situation, and perspective specific to it. Teachers of historical text are the students' guides in determining how to read and interpret that text, as it is very different from literary, scientific, or visual text. The tools that are needed in order to be successful in reading a particular type of text are not universally the same, and it is important to allow students the insight to realize and practice reading, evaluating and comprehending historical text as its own genre with its own strategies.

Scientific Texts

Texts read in a science lesson or classroom are content specific, and transacting with the text and co-constructing meaning is vital to the comprehension of this material. Much of the time, science text can be experiential, and includes labs and experiments that reinforce the material from the textbook, scientific research or journal. It is important, however, that when students encounter this type of text and material they take the time and are given the opportunity to transact, and make meaning with what the text means and what the new learning can do to add to their own understanding of the world. Science has the opportunity to engage students in hands-on learning, but the excitement of testing a hypothesis or learning about new scientific ideas can potentially limit the questions of "what does this mean to me?" or "why does this matter in my life?" Too often in science class, the answers to these questions are taken for granted, as all scientific learning pertains to the world around them and adds to their understanding of their environment. However, for students from the very young to the college-bound (and beyond) it is vital that they have the opportunity to add to the text of their own learning, and to make the meaning valid for their world as well as the larger world around them.

Math Texts

Reading in a math class is very specific and reflective of the content itself; many math teachers do not feel that they "do" reading in their class, or feel that there is a role that reading can practically play in their lessons. This is not the case at all. Math is a language all to itself, and teachers and students need significant time and practice to make meaning with math just as they do with reading any other content-specific text. The subject of reading, writing, speaking, and listening in a math class is itself deserving of an entire book, and we will not pretend to do it justice in the following section. But many lesson adaptations can be utilized to structure math-related reading activities that can support student learning and transacting in the classroom or lesson.

As with all reading, math instruction and comprehension is not memorizing facts; it is guiding students in investigations about math, mathematical concepts, and implementing programs that lead students to discover math, rather than just memorize its facts.

Performance and Art Based Classrooms Texts

Performance-based classrooms include drama, choral music, and dance. The performances and products are the texts in these classes, and those who experience them can transact with, interpret, and perceive (Eisner, 1985). Eisner's use of the term perception in the arts parallels Rosenblatt's term transaction and our term co-construction. Eisner contends that the perception of the art by each artist is what makes each performance or piece of art unique. An art teacher who asks each student in a class of 25 to paint a tree would expect many versions and perceptions of a tree. Similarly, a dance teacher who asked each student to choreograph a dance to the same piece of music would expect many different interpretations. These renditions are the artistic equivalent of students reacting to reading a novel, writing a short story, or analyzing a photograph. This is not simple recognition of what a tree is; rather, it is the interactive production and co-construction of what a tree looks like to each student.

Students should be encouraged to transact with these texts -- performances and products -- in any number of ways. For example, when they have seen a play, listened to a concert, or viewed a painting, students can write about, discuss, or illustrate their interpretations and share them with others. Students can also respond to written text through the arts.

Digital Texts

Much of the text that students encounter in today's world is digital: smartphones, computers, and tablets dominate the text-delivery method. The rules for interaction and transaction with these do not differ from other texts, but it is important for students to transact with them as they read them. Text is created more now than at any other time in history, and much of what students read today will never actually be printed. Twenty-first century skills — which are generally inclusive of reading and writing digital text and incorporating mostly digital text into everyday teaching and learning — are a major focus for today's teachers. It is imperative to include a discussion of this medium, as it continues to shift and change according to advances in technology as well as trends in the integration, teaching and learning of technology.

Many districts see the value of digital learning in their classes, and many more see emerging and evolving technology and resources as an essential part of modern teaching. Indeed, districts have spent many millions of dollars to embrace and incorporate technology into their curricula. Some have even decided to spend time and resources in 1:1 technology programs in which each student has a computer or tablet to use at school and/or at home on assignments. This expense can be stressful for teachers, who are pressured to include the technology in their classes every day and in every lesson. Textbook companies are including more and more digital resources in their textbook companions, and many textbooks are available with online versions in addition to the traditional print version.

The most effective use of technology in classrooms is not to require its implementation, but for districts to stress its importance to teachers, and even that it is preferred, but that they not feel compelled to include technology when the lesson is best taught without it. When districts and administrators allow teachers to make choices about what to use in their classroom, and which version of text to present to students, digital instruction becomes something that teachers see as enhancing learning rather than hindering it.

Using digital resources and asking students to read digital text requires that students understand its nature, and especially Web 2.0 tools. Tools that are considered Web 2.0 allow multiple users to contribute to and edit documents, repositories and websites, and therefore the validity of the text that they are reading must be considered as well.

Visual and Audio Texts

Up to this point we have been speaking of text in its more traditional role of written words on a page or in a document, but text is not only written words. Texts are also photographs, speeches, videos, podcasts, songs, and experiences that students engage with in their learning. Primary source documents such as maps, charts, graphs, and infographics are also text, and each type requires that students are supported in their learning so that they can continue to ask questions and make meaning, discuss with one another, and co-construct the learning as it occurs. Graphic organizers and analysis worksheets can further assist students in their understanding of these types of text, as well as multiple opportunities for students to make sense of their own learning, compare their understanding to that of their peers, and engage in a continuing and evolving conversation about the learning that is taking place.

Adaptations for Students with Different Learning Needs

Adapting lessons for students of all learning needs is not always limited to students with learning disabilities. All students can benefit from scaffolding and varying strategies of instruction, and the BDA format can help to support all students' understanding of text, no matter the grade or ability level of the students or the complexity of the text.

English Language Learners

Students for whom English is not their first language face additional challenges when transacting with text, as they first need to learn to comprehend the text in order to make sense of it. A co-constructive classroom surrounded with the Five Reading, Writing, and Talking Processes allows students to make meaning and interact with the text, and to bring their own knowledge and experiences to the classroom and their own understanding. The prior knowledge of these students can be vastly different from that of their peers, and teachers who honor these students' knowledge and experiences can further extend a welcoming hand. Teachers also help to support students' understanding of English when they read to their classes from many and varied texts, and support self-selection in independent reading.

Students who are learning to speak English at school while speaking another language at home are straddling two worlds. Their native language should not be prohibited at school. Rather, these students should be allowed and encouraged to use their native language alongside English, especially as they make meaning and connect text with their lives. When English language learners investigate sentences and words in collaboration with other students, their vocabulary and vernacular increase significantly, and their ability to read for understanding also grows.

It is also important to note that vernacular for all students can be very different from Standard English. There is much debate surrounding English dialects, Standard English versus Non-Standard English usage and their appropriateness in the classroom. This is not a declaration of which side is right or wrong. However, it is important to understand that the goal of a co-constructivist classroom and the transactional nature of reading is that students are able to express themselves in ways that are comfortable to them. It is only when we meet students where they are that we are able to guide them to new learning and understanding of text and knowledge. When teachers do not accept student expressions based on their use of grammar, word choices, and other stylistic choices, students' voices are not only limited — they are altered, and the students are less able to make meaning, draw their own conclusions, and develop as learners and thinkers. When students are stigmatized they become fearful and timid learners who likely choose not to participate in classroom transactions and interactions. Below are a few ideas for discussing different types of language in the classroom.

When a student offers a sentence or word that is right for their vernacular but wrong for standard English, the teacher can say, "Yes, that's one way to say it, but what would another way be?" Teachers can offer students various personas to imitate, re-writing the sentence for each person (examples: news anchor, teacher, President, their own parent or another family member) Students can then discuss the appropriateness of each sentence, and determine which is most suitable for different scenarios.

Elementary

Transacting with text in an elementary classroom engages students in whole class, group, and independent reading activities. For pre-school students or children in kindergarten through second grade, these activities are often done with a lot of scaffolding and teacher support. Think-aloud activities occur when the teacher exposes their processing strategies by literally thinking their thoughts aloud. They might say something like, "After reading this section, I wonder if…," or they might describe looking at a picture and the steps they would take to figure out what is going on. The purpose of the think aloud is to give students the language and questions they can use in their own exploration of text. The teacher gives them powerful examples and the encouragement they need to think about text or ideas. Students who struggle to comprehend text or with certain aspects of reading can benefit greatly from hearing how someone else thinks; it allows them to absorb the suggested strategies into their own learning and day-to-day transactions.

Reading Series and Anthologies

Reading instruction in elementary schools can often be limited to reading series and anthologies, which level all readers to the supposed abilities of students within their grade level. The teacher guides for these reading series typically focus heavily on comprehension and, sadly, for preparing young students to take tests. Book publishers choose to present texts and accompanying activities that are frequently overly scripted, right-and-wrong-answer oriented, and lacking opportunities for creative expression and personal reflection. Companies do this to encourage their reader and teacher guides to be passed by state adoption committees that tend to be more conservative and biased towards materials that seem to "support" the current data-driven approach to learning. While students in a balanced literacy environment and less scripted teaching environment thrive — and generally do better on standardized tests — this type of teaching must be supported. Teachers need to be engaged in conversations and peer coaching, but many districts do not build this into their schedule due to the many time constraints of education and testing. The purpose of literature in a reading series should not be to serve as a vehicle for student testing; rather, it should be a vehicle for student learning, and front and center in the learning process. Its role should be to assist students in thinking about their world, not to practice answering questions on a test.

Read Alouds- Elementary

Reading aloud to students is an incredibly important activity at the elementary level; there may be none other that matches it. When possible, start the school day by reading aloud to students for the first ten or fifteen minutes of class without comment. At other times, ask the students open-ended questions like, "What stood out for you?" Teachers who read aloud from books that inspire give all students access to ideas from many genres of literary and informational texts. Many times this comes from books that the students cannot read themselves. The research is abundantly clear: the best readers are those whose parents or caretakers read to them and talked with them about books from their earliest days. Listening to and talking about texts develops interests, knowledge, interpretation, and vocabulary, as well as a sense of the melodies and rhythms in language not represented in text, and the motivation to read the texts themselves. Students who have not been as fortunate in their exposure to reading and books through their life must engage positively with text, and the classroom teacher — through the read-aloud — can offer this experience and exposure to all students, thus benefitting them all.

Read Alouds-Secondary

Reading aloud is generally thought of as an activity for elementary school. Students gather on a carpet or relax at their desks while the teacher reads aloud from a story or picture book. Seldom is it thought of as a staple in high school or even middle school classrooms. In about fourth or fifth grade, the majority of the texts that students read shifts abruptly from literary to nonfiction and the amount of text read aloud diminishes by more than half. Reading aloud to students, at all levels, should occur regularly if not daily — even in high school and across all subject areas. Hearing literature and informational texts (including students' work) read aloud gives all students access to more sophisticated and complex texts than may be handled independently. In addition, the teacher's role as interpreter and mediator enhances comprehension and shows the student readers what to do with texts, especially when they are challenging, whether linguistically, in content, or both. When teachers provide opportunities for students to interact with challenging text as they listen – whether to mark the text, ask questions, or compare experiences – they are providing the scaffolding that supports students in building more complex responses to the text. When teachers (rather than students) read aloud, students reading below grade level have more access to the text and to the content.

Reading text aloud can be a very productive activity for students at all grades. While they might not read as many picture books, middle and high school students benefit greatly when teachers read aloud on a regular basis. Some teachers begin each day reading a single poem, or a paragraph from a current news article or novel that may or may not relate to what students are learning in class. When the teacher reads aloud, students can focus on listening and reflecting on the content of the text without stumbling over difficult words and unfamiliar vocabulary pronunciation. Though students should also have many opportunities to read to themselves, not reading aloud is often a missed opportunity to show students a fluent reader's voice and to allow them to hear the text as the teacher believes it was meant to be experienced.

Reading storybooks and picture books at the middle and high school level can also give students a chance to develop interest in a particular topic and to see a simplified explanation of events, people, and topics of study. There are many resources for excellent children's books for use in the middle and high school classroom, including the National Council of Teachers of English (NCTE) award-winning books like the Orbis Pictus Award, Caldecott Award, and others.

Approaching Reading Tasks

Far too many students approach all reading tasks in the same way. They do not vary their approach to accommodate the type of text, task, or assignment. They have little awareness that they have a choice of reading strategies, and therefore have little investment or sense of control over their processes or outcomes. Becoming a strategic reader and learner means acquiring a repertoire of strategies and ways to approach text. It is critical that students have many opportunities to figure out how to go about reading different types of text, and each content-area teacher should support students in their approach to reading their particular text or kind of text. The science teacher is the expert in reading and writing science texts. The Civics teacher is similarly best suited to teach that type of text, and the Math teacher the math textbook.

As teachers create environments for learning in which reading is experienced as meaningful "transactions with text," there are a variety of activities that can support the co-constructive and transactional nature of reflecting on text. With adaptations, these activities can be used successfully with students of all ages and across the curriculum.

- **Discussions:** Informal, spontaneous sharing between/among pairs or small groups; structured discussion tasks designed for pairs, triads, and small groups; whole class discussions (led by teacher or students).

- **Enactments:** Oral and choral readings; role-playing, dramatizations (including pantomime, improvisation, simulation); discussions or debates.

- **Presentations:** Talks, speeches, oral reports, demonstrations, panels.

- **Writing:** literary and informational formats including retelling, questioning, making notes, and mapping.

- **Other Media:** Artistic (drawing, sculpting, constructing), musical and video.

All of these formats or activities involve some form of composing, whether oral or written, and may take place before, during, or after reading. When these activities occur after reading they may naturally lead to further activities. For example, if students share their reflections or summaries with one another, the can also discuss which of the summaries was most representative of the text, draw examples from the text, and enhance their own reflection based on the work of their peers. The discussions and enrichment activities that are done in response to other students' products or reflections can be the most helpful in supporting student learning beyond the assignment itself.

In the pages following this chapter, there are a number of activities that are described in greater depth, and which are great examples of Before, During and After Activities. Although some are more appropriate to literary and others to informational text, all encourage readers to become actively and meaningfully engaged with text.

Literacy is a complex, co-constructive process by which learners make meaning as they transact with texts, whether they are oral, experiential and written, or visual. This process starts at the beginning of life — it does not wait for a child to reach a certain age. Readers of all ages benefit from meaningful discussions and reflections on text, and that reflection can enhance the learning and allow the text to make sense in one's own life.

The fundamental aspect of meaning making is that what is created is not what is literal and found in the text, but what is fundamentally in readers' heads as a function of their genes, their histories, and their individual social backgrounds. Readers get the most out of texts when they are encouraged, enabled and coached in how to do it. Once they learn, they are better able to transact with imaginative, informational and persuasive ideas and texts. The BDA strategies offer adaptable teaching processes to support and enrich such transactions across the curriculum.

Chapter 6
Process 2: Composing Text

Writing should be meaningful for children. An intrinsic need should be aroused in them, and writing should be incorporated into a task that is necessary and relevant for life. Only then can we be certain that it will develop not as a matter of hand and finger habits, but as a really new and complex form of speech.

Lev Vygotsky

Remember that there is simply no substitute for writing every day to establish classroom structure. Through daily writing, (students) develop their rhythms, their rituals of getting work done, and their rituals of consultation.

Donald Graves

The second Reading, Writing and Talking Process centers on writing as an intellectual and social activity fundamental to learning in all content areas. Similar to reading, writing is a complex language process involving the construction, analysis, interpretation and communication of ideas.

Learners bring their prior knowledge, experience, beliefs and attitudes to their writing in both process and product. In the world, and ideally in their learning environments, writers write in varied contexts and for many purposes. Both process and product is important in writing, as they each reflect the settings, functions, audiences and the profoundly social nature of writing itself.

Learning to compose for different purposes and to select the methods most appropriate for these purposes is a key part of learning to write and writing to learn.

In elementary classrooms, the Writer's Workshop is an opportunity for students to make meaning through their writing as they choose their own topics, audiences and goals. Talking (composing oral language) and writing (composing written language) are abilities that emerge early in young children, and are enhanced through guided and independent processes. Communication and talking begin early in children's lives. Their brains are "wired" for talk out of the need to communicate their wants and needs to their parents and caregivers. When students come to school, their oral language is advanced and remarkable. Children sound like the other members of their families and communities. They have vocabularies of many thousands of words and interact easily with trusted friends and family. The extent to which they have a developed vocabulary significantly impacts their learning, and will be discussed in chapter 7, Extending Reading and Writing. Regardless of the size of a student's vocabulary, however, composing text is an important aspect of his or her development and learning in school.

By the time students come to school, they vary in the extent to which they have emerged as fledgling writers. Some students have greater control of their writing and enhanced vocabularies to propel their writing. Whatever they have experienced before, research has demonstrated that students who are given many opportunities to write in every subject and at every grade level are better writers than those who have had writing experiences that are limited in scope and topic. Thus, students who are given opportunities to choose their topics balanced with teacher directed topics grow and learn more as a result of that instruction. Students should be allowed to explore and try new things in their writing across all subjects. Writing for the sake of writing, especially in young children, can be an exceptional resource for the learner and for the process itself, and lends itself to much more authentic learning in both process and product.

Composing in a balanced literacy and learning program centers on writing as an intellectual and social activity, fundamental to learning in all content areas. Writing is a complex language process involving the construction, analysis, interpretation and communication of ideas. Learners bring their prior knowledge, experiences, beliefs and attitudes to their writing. When students are encouraged to share their writing, they inspire one another to become better writers. This expands the entire class' exposure to different styles of writing and provides students with opportunities to share their writing.

In the world, and ideally in the learning environments of the school, writers write in varied contexts and for varied purposes. Their composing processes and products reflect the particular settings, functions and audiences for their writing and the profoundly social nature of writing itself. Learning to compose for different purposes, and to select the processes most appropriate for these purposes, is a key part of learning to write and writing to learn.

Learning to write is an easy concept to understand; writing to learn is somewhat more complex. Learning to write can touch on both the physicality of students learning to hold a pen or pencil or type on a keyboard to write, as well as on learning the conventions and grammar of writing effectively. They develop the skills to help them succeed in their writing. When students write to learn, they engage in the writing to help them understand, process, and deepen their knowledge about a particular subject. Sometimes, the simple act of writing down one's ideas can help to strengthen, clarify and even expose ideas that the student had not realized he or she even had; the act of writing intensifies the learning and reinforces the writers' ideas. Writing to learn is a valuable and widely untapped teaching approach. It must be structured enough for students to understand its goal, but unstructured enough that they don't focus so heavily on the task that they forego the actual learning that their writing can elicit.

Curriculum and instruction influence powerful notions of what writing is and how it should be used. Instead of teaching writing as a technical skill to be mastered, schools need to provide personally meaningful opportunities for students to use writing for articulating, clarifying, critically examining, and remembering ideas in all the disciplines. This helps them make sense in and of their worlds. Students need to have many varied opportunities to write – for themselves, for their peers, for the teacher, and for other audiences outside the classroom.

Writers Across The Curriculum

All children come to school as composers. Regardless of the extent to which they have actually written words on a page and created stories, they have each participated in situations where spoken and written language was used for learning and communication. As they mature, students gradually acquire more sophisticated abilities of communicating using different systems of language. They do not all learn these new strategies and methods for communication in the same way. Learners vary in style as they interact with different situations and with the complex nature of the writing system itself. A writer's development is a social process; it is the result of complex interactions of individual learners' processes, the products they create, and the cultural contexts that affect what and how they learn.

The "technical skills" of writing are not easy to discuss. American schools have a long history of teaching writing through discrete exercises, and of teachers assigning and then correcting writing. They focus on the products of writing rather than paying attention to writers' efforts and the meaning making that occurs through the process of learning to write and the craft of writing itself. There is a heavy focus, especially in the middle and secondary grades, on grammatical and mechanical errors and on fixing those errors. The general attitude is that student writing is a burden — a huge pile of papers to correct and return — and this has been a central problem of teaching for a long time. Teachers are hesitant to assign more writing simply because they don't have the time to grade the assignments. Think about a high school where each teacher instructs seven sections of thirty students each per day. If teachers assign just one additional paragraph of writing for each student, this equals approximately ninety pages of double spaced, 12-point font text for them to grade. Assuming that it takes a minute and a half to read each page of typed text, this means adding approximately two hours and fifteen minutes of work. It should come as no surprise that teachers are hesitant to assign more writing; doing so means assigning themselves hours of additional homework.

Writing for writing's sake is an important value to teach students. It is not necessary to grade all student writing; to do so would be burdensome to both the teacher and to the student, and nearly impossible for the teacher to manage. It would be a disservice to teach students that the only writing that matters is the writing graded by their teachers. Indeed, students need to learn to write for themselves, for their own understanding, and for their own independent purposes.

Many myths about writing, the writing process, and the nature of writing itself can be challenging for students and teachers to overcome. These myths include the necessity of needing to know what you are going to say before you begin to write and the idea that there's a right way and a wrong way to write. These ideas are pervasive, and hinder the writing process for students.

Composing is a powerful learning process that helps students relate new information to the known and to connect their experiences and prior knowledge with the subjects they study. Through various types of writing, students put the language of text into their own words, processing ideas meaningfully and deeply so that they can think about and remember them. Writing can slow thinking down, so it is important for teachers to allow students more time for planning and reflection. Through self-paced trial and error, a student will grow and learn as a writer.

Types of Writing

Much of the writing done in school involves students writing to answer questions, to record information, or to demonstrate the acquisition of knowledge. Too often the sole audience for a student's writing is the teacher. Learners need opportunities to write for a variety of purposes with a range of topics and audiences.

The goal then, for teachers of all ages and content areas, is to create a classroom environment in which students can write consistently. This allows them to refine their understanding and command of the writing process as well as of writing conventions. Student writing is one of the most productive ways of getting all students to construct meaning by using language. It makes it possible for all students to be engaged in their learning. Writing also helps students make sense of intellectually demanding ideas and topics and to voice their opinions about these ideas in expressive, informational and poetic ways. While student writing might intersect through these three categories, they represent most writing that students construct.

Expressive or Personal Writing

Students compose expressive writing with themselves as their main audience. The goal of this writing is to record information from observation, listening, or reading. It helps them to discover ideas, to clarify thinking, and to express emotions. Expressive writing can be understood as thinking aloud on paper, and writers often use expressive writing freely and spontaneously. Examples of this include diaries, journals or blogs in which students note and explore their perceptions of facts, opinions and feelings. This kind of composing is commonly unstructured, as this type of writing is used more to explore ideas rather than to shape and present them.

Students need daily opportunities to write spontaneously and expressively to explore ideas and responses. There are many ways to incorporate writing into the curriculum without taking away from instructional time. This is an important point, as teachers often cite a lack of instructional time as a reason for not including more writing in their curriculum. Instead of asking students to discuss something, teachers can instead ask them to write a response and share it with a neighbor. This builds writing into the curriculum and allows all students to participate actively in the learning and transacting, whereas oral conversation may be dominated by just a few. Instead of (or in addition to) using short answers or fill-in-the blanks, teachers can ask students to write a response to an open ended question. Instead of asking students to passively read or watch a video, they can use writing to record their impressions, identify their problems in understanding and pose questions for further study. This writing does not need to happen each time, but adding writing assignments that are used solely in conjunction with learning can allow the students to practice their writing in varied, authentic purposes, building both the habit and the stamina for writing in various forms and for a variety of purposes. These purposes should also include writing assignments that are focused on content learning, which can help students learn to write in varied ways and for authentic purposes building both the habit and the stamina for writing.

Informational or Transactional Writing

Informational writing includes language used to inform, record, report, advise, explain, instruct, theorize and/or persuade and typically has a thesis or main topic to focus the writing. This kind of writing uses language to act on the facts and perceptions of the individual student, and is typically more common of the type of writing that students are assigned to complete and is more common in school.

Poetic or Creative Writing

Poetic writing uses language as an art medium; it can be considered an artistic representation of thoughts and ideas using language as the medium. The purpose of this kind of writing is to entertain and/or to present ideas artistically, through many types of writing, including poetry, narrative writing, and other genres. These patterns include the sounds of the language, the writer's feelings and ideas, and events that the writer discusses as well.

The following chart lists some of the types of texts described in the three categories above. The chart is not meant to be exhaustive, and some writing types appear in more than one category. Drafts of the same texts could conceivably move from one column to another. What is most notable is the potential for learning that is inherent in the different functions of text and types of writing.

Functions and Types of Writing Across the Curriculum		
Expressive	**Informational**	**Poetic**
Notes	Reports	Poems
Journals	Editorials	Stories
Diaries	Commentaries	Songs
Letters	Essays	Letters
Logs	Interviews	Posters
Double-Entry	Autobiographies	Plays
Notebooks	Maps	Novels
Writer's Notebooks	Diagrams	Interviews

The Writing Process

Student writers need many opportunities to experience and experiment with different types and genres of composing in meaningful contexts across the curriculum. Many opportunities already exist in the daily curriculum for spontaneous, expressive writing to explore ideas and responses to experiences both in and out of the classroom. Instead of simply asking teachers to have students turn and talk, teachers can ask students to write their ideas and then share them with their partner. John Collins (2012) refers to writing as thinking on paper, and many opportunities for such thinking and reflecting occur in a student's every day school experience. Students should have between ten and twelve opportunities to write on a daily basis, including short writing tasks, particularly once they are in middle and high school. This promotes habit, fluency, and the focused practice that is necessary in order for them to grow and learn as a writer. Though much of the writing in this chapter is focused on longer assignments, there is much research that indicates that students benefit from short, focused writing activities that both engage the learner and promote critical thinking during the course of a lesson. This writing is not necessarily graded, nor must it always be collected. Including short writing opportunities for students can help students practice their writing, refine their craft, and continue to develop as readers, writers and thinkers.

The act of writing itself can be very challenging for students in many ways. If we expect them to become successful and confident writers, it is important that they write on a regular basis. Compare writing and composing to running a marathon. Completing the marathon is the end goal. No skilled runner would attempt to achieve this goal without extensive training, and no inexperienced runner would opt to run a marathon as his or her first attempt at running. Students need training and practice as they move to accomplish their educational goals, and writing is no exception — rather, it is the shining example of how practice and training is necessary for students to become successful and to achieve their learning goals.

True learning is not passive, and writing is a concrete way to make that learning active for all students. Instead of calling on one student for a response, teachers can opt to have all students write their response to a question. This opportunity for writing builds wait-time into teacher questioning, and allows additional processing time for students who need it. When the teacher then calls on a student at random, there is a better chance that they will have a response. This technique takes very little instructional time from the teacher, but provides for much more active learning for all students rather than only the student who was called on. Classroom-based writing builds stamina and habit, and allows students to practice writing multiple times. These informal, spontaneous writing opportunities, in addition to formal writing assignments, can extend and deepen students' grasp of subject matter and provide the opportunity for higher-level thinking.

Neither discrete nor linear, the writing processes described below suggest some of the implications of writing theory across the curriculum. These are dimensions and aspects of composing, not steps or stages in a single composing process. Therefore, not all writing needs to complete all steps, not all writers benefit from all steps, and some of the steps can be completed out of the order below based on the teacher, students and assignment.

Additionally, each of these stages can be completed using various teaching and writing strategies, both with and without the use of technology.

Getting Started: Pre-writing, Invention and Planning

Pre-writing has been used as a universal term for experiences that precede or motivate writing, but the term is in some ways a misnomer. It is not really "pre" or "before" writing, but rather uses writing to generate and/or explore ideas, to plan, and to rehearse. In reality, all of our experiences may be considered 'pre-writing' since we compose to makes sense of the world all of the time. Writing and writing assignments may evolve from shared experiences in the classroom that involve talking and listening. A small group discussion of a story is a pre-writing activity. Students discuss what they have read and then write about what they have discussed.

When teachers understand pre-writing as a fluid and on-going process that is intrinsic to life in the classroom, it releases them from feeling that they need to artificially stimulate and stage events in order to motivate and activate students. Students already have many things to write about: their lives and experiences outside of school, life in their classroom community, the ideas and texts that are studied in their classrooms, and content-specific ideas in the areas of literature, social studies, science, mathematics and other subjects.

Pre-writing must be taught and explained in a way that makes sense to students and helps them see its potential. From very early grades through high school, students benefit when teachers take the opportunity to show them how to jot, question, and make notes from listening and reading, as well as to brainstorm, keep journals, map, and other tools that writers invent and use to understand and explore ideas through writing. These benefits can be demonstrated and modeled through Think-Alouds, group brainstorming, and other activities that allow students to practice pre-writing as a part of and connected to the content that they are learning rather than as a separate strategy without any association to relevant content. These pre-writing activities can also be helpful for students in revising or reworking a text <u>after</u> they have written a first draft.

When teachers begin treating pre-writing as ongoing, students start to see that writers write all the time. This can have a profound impact on students with negative attitudes about writing as they begin to see that their experiences, as well as their reactions to these experiences, can be compositional. The documenting of these experiences in either digital or handwritten compositions can be an easier transition if students think of their inner monologue as the text from which they can initially write.

In this sense, pre-writing is as much an attitude as it is a process. Teachers in every subject area need to nurture students' abilities as talkers and writers. Every class needs to become a place where students can be writers: learning to and from composing, and encouraging play, speculation and tentativeness. Drafting and pre-writing activities are excellent ways to show students that the composing process can be both informative and creative, and can be used as a helpful strategy for learning.

Revising

Revising is best when it is a continuous process of reviewing, re-envisioning, re-starting and re-making that helps students understand their subject and generate ideas. Young children often revise by adding to whatever they have previously written. This writing can help to develop their voices as storytellers, to incorporate new grammar such as capital letters and new sight words, or to work on story development. Later, students may learn to play with their writing by using the words they originally wrote to change or reorder the story and create something new. Students often complete a writing task and assume that it is a finished product; they may not want to "mess up" their draft by adding to it or changing anything. Teachers can show students samples of their own drafts or even work done by another student so they can see how messy revisions can be.

Revising often occurs in response to information from peers and the teacher about how the draft meets readers' expectations and generates specific questions about the writing. Students are not always intrinsically motivated to revise their own work, and can be impacted by classroom input both positively and negatively. If the students understand the role and importance of the revision process they are more likely to take advantage of the benefits of re-writing. Students who experience peer editing and revising that is not well supported by the teacher, or that is not valued by the atmosphere in the classroom, will be unlikely to take much from the experience — and high-achieving students may resent the process altogether.

Editing

Editing is different from revising, and is essential for texts that students want others to read and understand easily. Teachers should provide students with a limited number of rules for each writing assignment; this benefits both the teacher's grading and the students' focus in their writing. By focusing on two or three areas, students are better able to learn and apply new strategies. These areas can be as simple as "start each sentence with a capital letter" for younger elementary grades, to "support each argument with 2-3 facts". John Collins (2007) describes these rules as Focus Correction Areas, and emphasizes the role that they play in concentrating student effort in refining their writing skills.

Teachers can also support this editing through the Document Review Process which allows teachers to highlight specific areas of need that many students exhibit in their writing. They then create mini-lessons for the whole class to practice these particular skills in the context of their own writing. When students use their own writing (or that of their peers) to practice specific skills, the learning is more meaningful, and makes them more aware of the role that certain issues have on their own personal writing. This practice of teaching writing in the context of what is already being written in the classroom is more effective than teaching these same skills as a separate subject or set of exercises from a grammar workbook unconnected to the rest of the content or lessons already in progress.

While editing is an important aspect of composing, it should not be stressed prematurely or at the expense of drafting and revising. Students need to care about what they write before they can become invested in the way that they write it.

Publishing

Publishing means something different now than it did ten years ago. Today's publishing involves students sharing their writing in a number of ways; from online texts and blogs to wikis, from class websites to presentations. The potential for a text to reach au diences wider than the students' immediate community is real, and therefore publishing has a deeper, more profound impact than it used to. This publishing does not need to be limited to finished drafts. Students can publish their writing in progress for feedback and to help spur the imagination of others. Sharing can occur at any point in the composing process, so that students can "publish" their plans, their drafts, or their edited copies.

In the younger grades, publishing can also mean taking students' writing portfolios home to share with parents and other family members. This portfolio can include work that students create with their classmates as collaborative writing assignments or a sampling of their writing as they complete it, showing the development of their writing skills, penmanship, stories, illustrations and revisions throughout the year. A first grade portfolio can include one story and one informational piece from the beginning, middle and end of the term, to be presented to parents at the end of the school year.

Final drafts can be published within a class by giving students the opportunity to read each other's papers, listen to papers read aloud, create booklets or collections of work, and/or post or display their writing. It can also be done online through any number of websites and apps, allowing the audience to expand beyond the students' immediate school community. These activities can also extend across the same teacher's classes, or between thex middle or upper grades. Collaborative projects between older and younger students widen the audience for student writing and have a dramatic effect on student attitudes, as well as on the quality of writing that the students produce. Publishing across grades can be accomplished through the use of display cases throughout the school, having work appear in the school magazine or newspaper, cross-grade letter writing or writers' assemblies, and collaborative projects between older and younger students.

Other options for sharing include setting up poetry readings, dramatic performances or collaborative publications like grade level newspapers for students and parents. Widening the audience for student writing beyond the teacher, in all of the ways described above and many others not mentioned, has a dramatic effect on student attitudes and on the quality of the writing produced. For each, the writer's process in composing reflects their own selection among a range of options based on their purpose for writing, the genre or type of writing, and their intended audience. Learning to choose a topic, type of writing, the audience and process is part of acquiring a composing repertoire.

Constructing Writing Assignments

Teacher-designed writing assignments can range from one extreme to the other —from completely open (students find their own subjects, genre, audience) to completely closed (every choice is pre-determined by the teacher). What lies between those extremes is a lot of potential for variety, and most teachers include varying degrees of open and closed assignments. The most critical aspect of the writing assignment — regardless of whether the choices are the teachers' or students' — is the extent to which the writing is real and purposeful. If the assignment is simply inserted, without any connection to the class or its content, it lacks authenticity and students are less likely to buy into the assignment itself. Though not every writing assignment can be completely integrated into the class and the context of the content, when they are integrated, the writing takes on a different level of authenticity and purpose.

A great way to increase student writing in upper elementary through high school is with bell-ringer activities, which ask students to begin each day's class by writing. These assignments are typically already posted on the board when students arrive in class. Some teachers post writing prompts that have no relation to the actual content of the class they teach, but rather ask students to write about things that are simply interesting. While these kinds of assignments play a very important role in student writing, the teacher can instead pose a question that connects with a learning goal for the day. When the bell-ringer activity and writing task is connected to a lesson that the teacher is planning for that day, the writing opportunity provides two purposes: integrating writing into the lesson and providing students with a context for their lesson. This helps students to either prepare for the lesson by activating the Meaning Centered Lens or allows them to explore their thoughts related to an important part of the day's lesson. In this way, the teacher is preparing students for the lesson that will follow while also providing opportunities for open-ended questioning and a variety of writing types.

Ultimately, the quality of each assignment depends on the connectedness of the class content and the assignment. Teachers who practice Backward Design (Wiggins, McTighe, 2005) create assignments and design curriculum with an end result and goal in mind. This helps to streamline the writing, the process, and the content into an integrated plan that helps students develop writing skills along with learning the class content.

Teachers can ask students to interact with text through their writing and prompt student connections and transactions in many ways. They can ask students to use writing to

- Connect known ideas and concepts with new learning from class,
- Reconstruct new knowledge and use it in some way,
- Communicate meaning rather than display or regurgitate facts.

One of the most important aspects of choosing and designing a writing assignment is determining the extent to which students will be able to make their own choices about their writing.

Topic Ownership

When people own something, they tend to look after it and care for it. The same is true with writing. From the first day of school, when it is appropriate and reasonable within the curriculum, teachers must establish a classroom environment that values student choice in writing. Instead of assigning each fifth grader a historical figure from the Revolutionary War to research, allow them to choose which figure to write about for themselves. Choice influences student attitudes toward writing more than any other aspect of the teacher's writing program. When students choose their own topic and show genuine interest, they write more and are more excited. This leads to better quality writing, more in-depth products, and more enjoyable experiences for both the teachers and the students. Students who are invested in the topic they write about are more likely to spend time outside of school on their assignments, and there is a higher likelihood that the writing will make its way into the students' long-term memory. Teachers, similarly, invest more of their time and effort into teaching something that they care deeply about than is true of something that they include only because it is required by their curriculum.

Free choice is not always an option. When a classroom follows a highly specific curriculum, managed choice, or limited choice provides a great option for students at all levels. It provides choice within certain parameters, while allowing students to exercise some control over their writing or research topic, even though they must choose something that fits within that criteria.

The teacher needs to hold to the belief that students have lived long enough and observed the world enough to have something to say about it. What's more, they have to value all writers' expressions because they are unique to each of the students -- no one views the world in quite the same way. The teacher has to hold to this belief, even though some students may have difficulty hearing their own inner voice and giving it expression.

Different students require different strategies. Some seem to have readily available mental pathways to what they think and feel, while some seem unaccustomed to hearing their inner voice. These students may not understand the instructions, and teachers need to provide significant support and scaffolding to assist students in all aspects of the composing process, especially in their choices and narrowing of topics for their writing.

One suggestion is to invite one of the more able students to make a list of topics. As the class watches, invite the student to tell you what interests him or her, and write a list on the board, encouraging the student to continue until there are five to ten items. You might have to prompt the student with questions such as, "Have you traveled anywhere recently? Is there a member of your family you might want to write about? What is your favorite animal? What is your favorite story?"

When the student has come up with a list, he or she can prioritize the topics in the order he or she would like to write about first. After this demonstration, have the whole class do the same, making personal lists, then numbering the topics in the order of their preference. Staple the list to the inside of their writing folders. This can be done as a group activity as well, and the teacher can model the activity for the class and create a class list of topics in addition to the topics that each student selects.

By the time they are in third grade, students are aware of their audience of peers and what they would like to read. Topics are sometimes chosen because of their popularity. A teacher may also dedicate a poster in the room for students to add topics for writing as they think of new ones.

Brian Sutton-Smith and his colleagues (1982) conducted a worldwide study of the development of children's narrative competence by asking many preschool and elementary grade children to tell them stories. He wrote:

> *The most important curriculum conclusion from this study can be stated simply and directly. If you keep asking children to make up stories for you and show some delight at the stories they tell; and if you keep coming back and asking for more stories, then the stories get better and better. There appears to be clear signs of an increase in their narrative competence just because you have been a good and rewarding listener.*

> *Children also progress from telling you stories to wanting to write their own stories (Sutton-Smith, 1975).*

Sutton-Smith's findings support teachers who show acceptance and encouragement of their students' expressions. Parents and aides can be enlisted for this story taking, including asking students to tell stories, to "pretend read" based on the pictures or memory of the stories, telling a story based on a picture book, telling a story about a picture they have made and then writing what they say so they can copy it, and telling stories that the adult can record for them.

Integrating Writing with Reading

The Before-During-After Framework applies to Composing Text in the same way that it applies to Transacting with Text, as it highlights the many uses of writing across the curriculum. The role of writing when it connects to reading is aimed to help students make connections with the text. It makes sense of the text in relation to the rest of their learning, and supports the students in remembering what they read through their text-related writing.

Writing gives all students the opportunity to become actively involved, and that is the most important facet of the writing they do before and during reading. Writing engages all learners simultaneously, and allows an entire group to focus on and think about the matter at hand. When the teacher engages a class with a whole group discussion, many students play a passive role. Turning and talking with a partner to share ideas is a way to increase student engagement and allow each student to have a role in the class discussion. Incorporating writing is another way to increase student engagement. Simply engaging students in a brief jotting or listing activity during the discussion makes every student a potential contributor. When the responses of the group are pooled or shared, teachers often find that it improves the quality of discussion and increases the number of students who participate. Pre-reading activities that ask students to write often motivate less able readers, preparing them to read. Pre-writing can also demonstrate expertise and highlight prior experiences in the group as a whole. Without it, classroom discussions are often limited to the few students in the group who regularly participate orally and who are comfortable with this whole group approach.

Students' active use of language ensures a high level of meaningful involvement and participation in the class, and the likelihood of better comprehension and retention of the material taught. In addition, writing activities such as these require that everyone think about the material, not just the student who is called upon to contribute.

The strategies for using writing before, during and after reading are designed in part to alter the traditional set of roles in the classroom. No longer is the teacher the one asking questions and the students answering questions. Many of the pre-reading writing activities are designed to help the students question what they already know and to prepare them to raise their own questions while reading. This strategy emphasizes the importance of student-generated questions, and gives students a voice. Learning to question the text and their own learning requires that students compose questions and practice comprehending and responding to the questions of their peers. Good writing reflects the author's awareness of important (or surprising or useful) questions and writing topics. See Reading, Writing and Talking Process Five: Learning to Learn for more discussion about student self-questioning as a central process of learning how to be a good writer and learner.

To create successful writing activities, it is important to establish criteria for marking and grading an assignment prior to distributing it to students. Rubrics can be an efficient way to organize expectations. They streamline teacher responses to grading — even with very young children — and allow students to understand the expectations at the beginning of an assignment. Rubrics should not be overwhelming, overly complicated or unnecessarily detailed, but they should focus on two to three main areas, as Collins emphasizes through his Focus Correction Areas (2007).

Responding to Writing

One of the most daunting parts of assigning writing, particularly in the upper grades, is the need to grade and respond to all writing. The truth about writing (at all levels) is that students should be writing much more than teachers grade. When students are assigned longer, or more involved writing assignments, it exponentially multiplies the amount of time that teachers need to respond to and grade these assignments. Below are just a few tips for teachers looking to validate student writing and ensure that students feel they're writing for a legitimate purpose. Much depends on the structure of the schedule and the number of students that are enrolled in class.

Written Comments

Teachers' comments can play a powerful role in developing students' writing abilities. Students often begin to define themselves as writers as a result of those responses. Ironically though, most of the commenting that teachers are trained to do actually interferes with writing. Many times teacher's comments — especially those written in response to first drafts — may take the student's attention away from his or her own purpose, focusing on mechanical issues rather than substantive changes to content and topic. The student makes the suggested changes at the request of the teacher rather than because he or she has identified a need to revise the text and planned a strategy for revisiting.

Another problem, especially in the upper grades, is that many teachers' comments are often vague, such as "avoid passive," be more specific," and "awkward". Revising in this case becomes a guessing game of what the teacher wants. Worse yet is when the teacher re-writes student work in order for it to more closely say what they want the student to write, or what the teacher expects. When this happens, teachers take on the role of composer, preventing students from learning the art of revising or investigating his or her own writing. It can be frustrating to know what the student is trying to say, and though composing it for them can occasionally be helpful for students who struggle with finding their own written voice, doing so puts the teacher into the role of diagnostician rather than co-investigator. Here are some useful comments on first and later drafts.

First Drafts:

1. Respond to what seems to be the student's intended purposes and ideas.

2. Raise questions for the writer.

3. Make suggestions for a process for revising – something to do that will help move the writing forward.

4. Identify strengths and show how to build on them.

5. Ask students about the kind of feedback they would like.

6. Limit comments to a few concerns for each student.

Later Drafts:

1. Comment on the quality of the ideas, the organization, use of language etc.

2. Point to parts that seem to be working well.

Students can maintain writing folders — either digitally or physically in the classroom — that contain multiple drafts of their writing. When each piece is dated and kept in order, it provides them with a running record of their writing and how it has improved over a period of time. This folder can also record specific writing skills and strategies that have been addressed, including specific grammatical problems and mini lessons or cheat sheets to help them remember what they learned about writing in class.

Responding to Writing in Student Conferences

Conferences provide great feedback on writing for students at all grade levels. The structure of a student-teacher conference varies depending on the level and needs of each particular student, and this is the beauty of the conference: it allows teachers to teach composing to students at their own instructional level and to their own particular needs. Unfortunately, time limits the amount of conferencing that a teacher is able to support in the classroom. Teachers can set up rotating schedules at the elementary level, while middle and high school teachers can use online tools to augment their conferencing. This allows the conversation about writing to take place online in addition to face-to-face meetings.

Elementary Conferences on Revising

Conferences look different at all grades, as students at each age and level have discrete and unique needs that vary as they mature and develop into more skilled and capable writers. First graders begin revising at the level of spelling and story. As they continue to learn more and more sight words throughout the school year, they are likely to revise the words they use to the new words they have learned. As they become more familiar with the mechanics and forms of writing they will develop their revising skills, but need time and support to implement new writing skills. The revising instruction that most benefits students at this grade level is to prompt them to add one more fact or event to their story, or to end each sentence with a proper punctuation mark.

Third graders and above engage in more advanced revisions such as inserting paragraphs and rearranging whole selections. These students think more about revisions when they are away from school. They are able to do multiple drafts of a particular piece of writing and to apply revisions and re-writings to each draft. Teachers in second grade and beyond can establish a conference cycle for students, spreading out the conferences to make the process more manageable for teachers to realistically implement. Though teachers may assign each student a particular day for his or her conference, it is a good idea to also allow students to sign up for a meeting when they want to talk about their writing, with specific limits (for example, 2 per week) if necessary. Conferences are best done as part of a class activity that involves stations, with the conference being one of the stations where small groups of students can take turns meeting with the teacher for a few minutes while the others in the group engage in an alternate activity.

Conference logs can be extremely helpful, especially during parent teacher conferences and in developing mini lessons. They are also helpful if a student is feeling badly about his or her writing at a particular time; they give the teacher a record of all of the gains that the student has made throughout the year. For example, the teacher might remind the student about a great story that he or she wrote the previous month, and be able to cite the specific strengths of the story. In many classrooms, the number of students assigned to each teacher makes remembering such details unrealistic. The log allows the student to be the focus of the time that the teacher is able to set aside and provides him or her with an accurate record from which to draw.

Though the actual process will vary depending on the age and needs of the students, the following description can provide a general outline of a student conference:

At the start of the conference, students describe what their compositions are about, where they are in the process of writing, and what they plan to do next. If it's not too long, the student can read his or her composition aloud. The teacher then comments positively on what he or she sees in the composition. Then the teacher can focus on one way to help the student develop the piece further. The focus should be on the story or topic itself rather than on mechanics or spelling. In fact, at this point all invented spellings and other mechanical problems can be ignored, as this process is about drawing the student out into the writing as freely as possible.

If the students stories are abbreviated and lacking specifics, the teacher can ask them to probe for more elaboration and memories. Questions that are open ended can help to draw students into their writing, and continue to be the voice in their composition. Powerful questions include:

- "What got you interested in that subject?"
- "What would you like to add to your story?"
- "Where do you think the new information fits?"
- "Do you really want to keep this?"

Some students write the equivalent of a "bed-to-bed" story. The student writes the story of a main character and describes everything that the main character does from the moment he or she gets up until bedtime. It is helpful for teachers to try and focus students on the part of the story they care most about, and highlight those parts for the students to see as they revise.

Some students find it difficult to reach closure with a piece of writing; they continue to draft and rework it. While these revisions are wonderful practice, giving the students a deadline can help them to see the end of the tunnel and to find their conclusion. If they struggle with the end of the writing, either because they love the story and want to write more or because they are unhappy with their ending, you can encourage them to continue their writing during writer's workshop; but it is also advisable to insist that they find their closure so they can practice the end as well as the beginning and middle of their writing processes.

When students bring strong pieces of writing that express their views of the world vividly and accurately, teachers can focus on the positive aspects of the writing and ask students what they liked most about it. There is no need to find fault within each piece; in fact, it can be demoralizing for students to see what they may consider mistakes. Though there is always something that can be improved and revised, students who see their work as complete and who have met or surpassed the goals of the assignment can spend time discussing what they learned from the writing, or what they want to write next based on this writing experience. Each student should be able to experience positive writing conferences throughout the year, and the feeling of being successful writers.

Secondary Conferences on Revising

Writing conferences in middle and high school can be one-on-one (teacher-student or student-student), small group (peers), or whole group (teacher conferences in front of the whole class). Conferences that focus on informational compositions would proceed differently than conferences on literary text, which are also different from short stories and poetry. In each scenario, the teacher-student conference should first focus on the content and topic before shifting to an emphasis on the mechanics of the writing. While this can be especially difficult for high school teachers, spelling, grammatical issues and paper formatting should be mostly ignored in the initial conference on revision. As students become more familiar with the conferencing process, the teacher can set expectations for the student, or ask that students come to the conference with a specific goal or agenda. This helps to guide the conversation and increases the likelihood that the writer comes with the purpose of learning something rather than merely complying with the teacher's agenda.

Students can also learn to have meaningful conferences with their peers, and engage in productive discussions about their learning in pairs or small groups. This peer coaching — or editing — allows students to sample each other's writing, learn more about how their classmates organize their writing, and be exposed to different writing styles which may or may not impact their own. It is important, however, that students are given plenty of practice and modeling on how to use these conferences effectively so that they do not turn into a chorus of "that was good" without any concrete or constructive feedback to help each other in the revision and development of their work.

In order to support peer conferences, teachers can model effective conferencing strategies with willing participants, or stage "fish bowl" demonstrations of revision conferences to train students in helping to revise their classmates' work. These fish bowl activities can focus on any aspect of the writing process, with the main goal of helping to make students aware of how to listen and how to comment.

During the conference the writer reads his or her work to peers for comment and questions. When the students listen to their classmate rather than reading the text, they can focus on the composition's content. Students learn how to be good listeners by observing the teacher during the conference. The teacher can initially provide a list of possible prompts to help students learn to provide positive feedback and ask helpful questions, then add student contributions to these as the class develops more comfort with the peer-editing process.

The Writer's Workshop in Elementary Classrooms

One of the most effective ways to establish a culture of writing and to support the writing process, especially in an elementary classroom, is through Writer's Workshop. Writer's Workshop is a designated and consistent time when students are encouraged to think of themselves as writers, most frequently finding their own topics and stories. This workshop typically lasts about an hour at a time, and is a dedicated class time in which students can write and review completed writing assignments and research new topics on which to write. Students can maintain a Writer's Notebook in which they list their writing ideas from multiple sources, such as questions and ideas from reading, interesting experiences, things they observe in nature, events they learn about through school, and personal friendships and family interactions among others. They can brainstorm these ideas with partners and refer to their lists when they are deciding on a new topic or determining what to add to a work in progress. This notebook can help students to think of themselves as authors and reporters.

In addition to each student's notebook, students benefit from having access to a variety of writing styles and genres to which they can refer if they have a particular goal in mind. These texts serve as Mentor Texts, as they provide a model for various writing styles and techniques. These mentor texts can be very helpful in providing students with support and scaffolding as they try something new. Mentor texts can be located in a central area that can be a Writing Center for students to use and refer to throughout the Writers Workshop, and while writing to complete teacher-directed writing assignments as well.

The Writing Center

The Writing Center should be a specific area of the classroom that is designed to both stimulate and support the writing process. Items to include in a writing center include a word wall with focused vocabulary, writing folders for each student, lined paper, unlined paper, crayons, pencils and pens, computer(s), dictionaries, and other tools that support writing and illustrating. There should be pictures that depict standard forms for writing, for example:

1. A sample story or report which shows the following: a margin on the left side so pages can be stapled into books if necessary; writing on every other line to facilitate revision and editing; a place for a name, date and title and indentation for paragraphs

2. A sample friendly or business letter.

3. A sample conversation which shows punctuation and paragraphing.

    For example:

> "The Halloween show is about to begin," Mary remarked.
>
> "Well," said George seriously, "just keep calm and quiet."
>
> "Why should I?" shouted Oscar.
>
> Mary whispered, "We're all trying to be calm."
>
> "Be quiet, Oscar!" hissed George. "You'll upset the little ones."

4. Posters that indicate common errors of usage. For example:

I do not.	I don't.
He does not.	He doesn't.
She does not	She doesn't.
You do not.	You don't.
They do not.	They don't.

Research/Report Writing

Researching and writing about research is a difficult but important genre for students to practice and master through their educational career. The problem, of course, is the matter of the trustworthiness of the sources, and therefore of their integration. For this reason, it is probably a good idea for the first research topic of the year to be done as a class, with the teacher closely guiding the interpretation of multiple texts. The teacher can model continual questioning that gets out the biases and evidential base of the authors.

While doing group research, teachers can guide students on the fundamental research processes of questioning, observing, interviewing, careful description, paraphrasing, selecting and note-making — not as separate skills, but rather for students to learn these processes for the purpose of doing good research.

It is important to remember that students tend to believe textbooks and other texts they read unless they have been guided to read critically. This process can be assisted with questions like those mentioned in the first Reading, Writing and Talking Process posted on a chart. Ideas include

- What stood out for me?
- What else have I read that this reminds me of?
- How do I feel about this story/informational piece?
- What questions do I have?
- What questions would I ask the author, illustrator or characters?
- What do I agree or disagree with?
- Where can I get more information or evidence?

Following such a guided group research experience, a very personal and accessible form of research is I-Search. Macrorie recommends (1) using the class or group for tips on how to study it (2) finding experts or authorities (of any age) and asking them for the most useful books, magazines, films etc.; thinking about the best way to interview people who know a lot about a subject (3) using both first-hand sources (people and events) and secondhand sources (books, newspapers, people talking about what others know or have done). A recommended format for writing up this search breaks with the conventional but provides for authentic recording of the experience as well as the findings in four parts. The writer writes (1) what I knew and didn't know about the topic when I started out (2) why I'm writing this paper – what difference it may make in my life (3) the story of the search and (4) what I learned or didn't. Macrorie recommends simplified documentation like that found in current scholarly journals.

Drawing and Talking

Donald Graves and his associates in New Hampshire schools observed that first grade children orally rehearse and draw their ideas throughout the writing process. They will draw first, then begin their writing, then return to their drawing, then start writing again. The drawing helps them gather and rehearse their ideas. First grade writers are quite vocal (which has been learned by placing sensitive microphones near them as they write). They say words, sound out words, rehearse, and reread to themselves as they write. They rehearse ideas and discuss procedural matters with peers as well. They discuss the piece before, during, and after they write. To stifle this hum of vocalization would be to stifle writing development. By the time they reach the third grade, students are vocalizing less, but it is surmised that the oral rehearsal has been internalized as "inner-speech." To structure the Writer's Workshop, the teacher seats the students so they can talk to each other as they write, and also helps them be available for consultation.

The Lead, the Guts and the Closing – Rehearsing Leads

In the public elementary school in New Hampshire where so much of Graves' research has been conducted, the terminology used to identify the parts of a piece of writing are likely to include "the lead," "the guts," and "the closing." When students approach third grade and are better able to distance themselves from their work, they may be encouraged to try an exercise of writing three different leads of the same composition. They decide which one is preferable, possibly in consultation with a peer or the teacher.

Regularly Scheduled Writer's Workshops Promote Rehearsal

Students who know they'll be writing every day begin to think about their compositions when they are away from school. They search for leads and think about their composition while riding the bus, watching T.V. or lying in bed because they know the next day they will be returning to their writing.

Writing a First Draft

The teacher directs students to use cheaper paper for first drafts and to write on every other line to facilitate revising. The task of the writer when writing the first draft – the one the teacher must help the students keep in focus – is to gather all the ideas from the pre-writing phase and put them down, writing from beginning to end non-stop. The writer must let the force of principal ideas or feeling drive the composition from beginning to end. To become distracted at this stage with handwriting, spelling, or polished sentences could cause the thread to be lost. The task of the writer at this stage of the writing process is to give the composition its general shape and unity.

Temporary or Invented Spellings and Conventions of Writing

Given encouragement, young children begin with squiggles that look like writing. They then proceed to strings of letter and symbols, which they use to assign sound and meaning. Readers who have reached a phonetic stage will use the names of the phonetic value of letter names to write words, which they can read back: LK for look, HM for home. These spellings are invented, and each time the child writes, they are re-invented.

Many teachers report that their first graders or lowest second graders are sometimes so anxious to spell words correctly, and are so busy asking for the spelling of words, that they can't keep their topics in mind. The best recourse is to tell them to invent a spelling for the word or leave a dash and to fix it after they get all their ideas down on paper.

Children should be supported for their temporary spellings and conventions of writing by trying to read them and celebrate good approximations. Some children's invented spellings will be impossible to figure out, so ask them to read aloud what they have written. It's helpful to copy what the child says above his or her spelling attempts.

Having students involved in "doing grammar" several times a week in sentence-making and word-making investigations, as proposed in Reading

Writing Talking Process Four: Investigating Language, will provide them with additional skill with regular spellings and sentence rules, both during and when they revise their drafts.

The Author's Chair

The Writer's Workshop might begin with a variation of the familiar sharing time. Students enjoy sitting in the Sharing or Author's Chair, where they talk about something they are thinking about, a work in progress or a completed piece. A productive option to the problem of having one student at a time sitting in the chair is to have them pair up to share their ideas and products with one another.

A Final Word

While all five of the Reading, Writing and Talking Processes propose ways that students should be writing across the curriculum, Composing Texts gives particular emphasis to writing characterized as a research based, guided writing process carried out in a Writer's Workshop. It most often involves students' self-selection of audiences, purposes and topics. In elementary-aged students, the best way to become a writer is to be exposed to many stories and different types of stories, to read a lot and emulate being a writer. This process can begin at any age, and the ability to read is not required for this to occur. Those skills need to develop, and gradual growth occurs over time. It is important to foster these skills through many opportunities to practice writing, which can occur in both structured and unstructured activities.

Chapter 7
Process 3: Extending Reading and Writing

I don't want children to analyze authors; they should enjoy them. What matters is the story, the series of incidents. Criticism is the province of age, not youth. They'll get to that soon enough. Let them build up a friendship with the writing world first.

-Robert Frost

There are ten ways to become better readers: **READ, READ, READ, READ, READ, READ, READ, READ, READ, READ.**

-Jane Heilman

Reading and writing are lifetime skills. The extent to which students choose to pursue reading and writing outside of the classroom depends heavily on the texts they choose to read, the way that they interact with texts helps to build their relationship with books. Though schools can support students in becoming lifetime readers and writers in many ways, perhaps what is most critical is how they support students in choosing their own texts. Allowing self-selection (as much as can be reasonably expected) provides students with opportunities to choose what they read and what they write, both in and out of school. Many times, self-selection is reserved for enrichment opportunities and is supplemental to the core curriculum in the classroom, but self-selection should be a staple in all areas of learning and integrated into the curriculum, to at least some extent. There are a number of ways that students can take control

115

of their reading in partnership with their teachers. Extending reading and writing into self-selection and choice should be a priority in schooling at all levels, for all learners.

Developing lifetime readers and writers depends on the interactions and interdependence of learners, teachers, parents, and community members. These social networks can help create an environment that fosters lifelong literacy in many ways: by structuring choice into the core curriculum allowing it to occur weekly, if not more often. By providing more and better resources with which students can interact; by helping students and parents connect more meaningfully around shared reading, writing and learning, and by designing whole school literacy events.

Given the current climate of education and the emphasis on rigorous testing across many grade levels and content areas, it is understandable that teachers feel overwhelmed by the sheer amount of content to be covered. It is because of this stress that schools need to strive to provide students with opportunities to pave their own paths in reading and writing. Choice is unlikely to exist in the absence of consistent and thoughtful implementation of self-selection through the content areas, and this must be a value shared at the school and district level. As difficult as it may be, a thoughtful and explicit emphasis on self selection is essential and needs to be properly supported in each classroom and with each student. While choice is not reasonable all of the time, it is particularly important to find ways to structure classrooms and courses so that students still exercise significant choice and control over portions of their own learning.

The evidence for self-selected reading and writing is quite substantial, as indicated in the research chapter and, in particular, in Daniel Fader's experimental study of middle school age boys reported in his book: *Hooked on Books (1976)* Two major themes emerged from the evidence: first, the impact of providing choice in reading and writing experiences in school as part of the regular program and second, assigning and encouraging self-selected reading and writing activities to be done out of school. Both themes build on the obvious relationships between choice and motivation. When students are offered choices, they care about what they choose to do. This relationship between choosing and caring leads students to feel as though they own an activity rather than simply doing it because someone else asked or told them to do so. Students who have no opportunity for choice in their school tend to resent the process, as do the people who are assigning the tasks. There is no self-determination, no ownership of the learning or the content. School tasks can even enhance a student's feeling of ownership by providing choices within a pre-determined structure. In addition to opportunities to choose, students need to have time and space to read and write without the requirement of assignments that usually go along with the reading or writing. This unstructured reading and writing can be daunting for teachers who literally need to leave students alone with their reading and writing without checking for comprehension, completion or content. Still, extending the reading and writing processes in this way provides students with the most positive feelings about reading and writing, and makes them more likely to continue with their reading and writing outside of school.

Students at the elementary level should experience self-selected reading and writing often. Allowing students to create positive relationships with books is a vital step in creating lifetime readers and writers. Students benefit when they become more independent and interdependent in choosing and sharing books across the curriculum. They need to choose books for their own purposes and to engage in conversations with their classmates and teachers about books and genres. They need opportunities to read many types of text in order to form their own understandings of themselves as readers and writers as well as their own strengths and weaknesses. In addition, students need time to read and write for their own purposes and at their own rates, and to respond to text in their own ways by talking, writing and through a variety of art forms.

Self-Selected Reader's and Writer's Workshops (Elementary and Middle School Classrooms)

The self-selection process is central to students buying in to their own abilities and interests as readers and writers. In elementary school settings this can be achieved through Reader's and Writer's Workshops that emphasize self-selection. There are many aspects of organizing and orchestrating classrooms that support these workshops.

Collaboration with a Librarian/Media Specialist

Teachers who utilize self-selection in their classrooms already know that their best resource and ally is their librarian/media specialist. These individuals are key to the successful implementation of these workshops. They know where to get books in timely and cost-effective ways, can help to streamline students' self-selection processes, instruct students to find their own books and resources, and help students find and develop their own tastes and exposure to reading. Debra Gnawed argues for developing rotating classroom libraries that are serviced by a strong central library. In her article published in The School Library Journal entitled, *The Rotating Library (2000),* she notes that classroom libraries are strengthened when they are linked to a professional library center. Classroom libraries are relatively static; they don't have the variety or depth possible when teachers have access to a central library of resources that can be shared among many classrooms or buildings. Librarians can support teachers to rotate classroom collections and provide teachers and students with easier access to a variety of books and resources.

If there is no librarian in the school, or if the library does not include enough books to distribute among the classrooms and teachers, grade levels and teams can collaborate to create various reading areas throughout the school in common areas. The public libraries can also be very helpful in obtaining and supporting classroom collections, and teachers can work with local libraries to maintain a variety of book choices within and among the classes and schools.

Once teachers obtain a number of books for their classroom library, it is very important to make this space an inviting and organized area that students can use quickly and efficiently. It is also helpful to establish expectations for the area and to make sure that students know what they are expected to do when they choose a book to read from the class collection. The best classroom collections include a wide range of reading levels, both at the grade/reading level expected of students in the class and then also below and above. It is also important to incorporate a wide variety of genres, including adventure, fantasy, science fiction, poetry, biography, fairy tales, non-fiction stories and sports. When possible, a classroom library should contain no fewer than 100-150 books. This is especially important in utilizing the school or district library to assist in maintaining and rotating this selection. Teachers can also keep books written by former and current students in their collection.

Supplementary reading in content areas at the middle and high school level can help connect the curriculum between content-specific classrooms, where it is common for some fragmentation to occur. For example, reading historical fiction while studying U.S. history or world history can help make facts learned in class more realistic and connected to students. Teachers and librarians can work together to generate supplementary reading lists of books — with a wide range of reading levels — to be used with thematic units across several disciplines. Integrating outside reading with the ongoing work of the class helps to avoid isolated book reports. Students can write about topics that link texts assigned in class to their own individual choices around a specific theme or subject.

The Workshop Itself

In order for self-selection and Reader's and Writer's Workshops to be successful, students need to understand the expectations of the workshop and become enthusiastic about the process. Many students begin to appreciate the chance to read and write what they want and for their own purposes. Teachers can support this in their classroom environment through conversations in which they discuss why reading and writing is important, fun, and enjoyable as well as informative.

Reader's and Writer's Workshop can be implemented by engaging classes in the following stages and suggestions:

1. At the beginning of each Reader's Workshop, the teacher introduces one or more of the books by reading from them or commenting about them. Books the teacher has read aloud often become very popular in the classroom and are frequently top student choices. Teachers can also invite other school or community members to introduce their favorite books to the students, either in person or through video, audio, or online resources where individuals share their favorite books.

2. The students select their own books to read. It is best to set a time limit for the choice period to make sure that students do not spend so much time choosing a book that they do not have enough time for the actual reading.

3. The class engages in independent reading. The length of time that students should be reading may begin at about 10 minutes and then gradually increase to about 30 minutes as students develop more reading endurance. **During the designated reading time it is important that everyone reads, including the teacher.** If students do not see their teacher reading, the value of the

workshop is diminished and students get the message that reading is just a school assignment.

4. Younger students who are still in the pre-reading and pretend-reading stages may be given the choice of reading picture books alone or sharing their book with a partner while talking in an audible whisper.

5. When appropriate, students should be allowed to read in comfortable places around the room — not just at their desks.

6. At the end of Reader's Workshop, students can voluntarily share something from their reading to the class. There should be no tests, no reports, and no grades!

7. Students can keep a brief record of books they have read in a section of their portfolios. This record might include: the title, author, date completed and a brief written comment such as what stood out for them or what was worth sharing.

Repeating the Reader's Workshop process three-to-five times a week can establish rhythms, expectations and reading and writing stamina for students.

Student-initiated writing, either in response to or independent of self-selected reading, can occur regularly in the middle and high school level without much teacher direction. Personal journals to record thoughts, ideas and experiences, as well as reading journals that describe students' responses to readings, are two examples of this type of independent writing. Students can also keep writer's notebooks to keep track of topics that they want to write about in the future, and learning logs where they record questions and observations based on their ongoing work in class. In all of these types of self-initiated writing experiences, students have control over the quantity of their writing and are invited to apply the same strategy for different purposes. In this way they develop their voice and stamina as a writer using different genres.

Implementing Self-Selection

Integrating 'self-selection' into the curriculum and including it on extended writing assignments takes time and the development of assignments that support these selections.

The most important aspect of this implementation is providing students with the time to engage in self-selection. If teachers dictate all aspects of learning, the joy of the learning itself is less likely to pervade students' educational experiences. Though curriculum, testing and content requirements are very demanding, it is important to plan times during the day when students are encouraged to select materials to read or are given opportunities to write. National reports such as *Becoming a Nation of Readers (1985)* recommended that by third grade, students should read independently for at least two hours each week. In addition, many literacy leaders recommend that students read independently for one hour a day.

The most effective and impactful way to facilitate this — especially for elementary students — is at the classroom level, where teachers can incorporate independent reading and writing into the design of their schedule and classroom activities. In addition to providing the time to read and write, it is also important to provide time for students to talk about their reading and to share their writing. Small group or whole class sharing sessions and journal writing help to create the social networks that motivate and sustain students.

Planning time for self-selected reading and writing involves a combination of quiet time for reading and writing and time for sharing, reading sections of books aloud, and other informal discussions about texts. No matter how time is allotted and worked into the curriculum, teachers can discuss the importance of these workshops in their classes, communicate with parents about the purposes and expectations of the processes, and provide suggestions for how parents can support self-selected reading and writing at home.

Self-selection can also be useful in out-of-school assignments, which can be either supplemental to or alternatives to self-selection in the classroom. While it is optimal for students to have the opportunity to self-select as a regular part of their class and learning (as described above), sometimes this cannot work. When out-of-school assignments are the only ways to support self-selection, these opportunities should be as widely available as possible. It is often the case that self-selection is supplemental to the reading done in class.

Homework and summer reading assignments are a great example of how to implement self-selection outside of the school day. In middle and high schools these programs are best supported on a departmental level or throughout the entire school. English, Social Studies and other content-area teachers can work collaboratively to develop suggested supplementary reading lists that connect with the class that comes next in the curricular sequence. If implemented during the school year, teachers can determine what books can support the learning from each unit or quarter and then assign students to select one or more books to read independently or with a small group of classmates.

The goal of this assignment should primarily be for enjoyment, but can also extend students' understandings of themes or topics from class. When supplemental independent reading is connected with core content, it broadens students' knowledge base and enriches the learning of all members of the classroom community. When teachers can help students connect their outside independent reading with assigned reading, students can make connections between the informational, thematic and stylistic aspects of the text read in different contexts.

For many teachers, assigning book reports seems like a rite of passage. These assignments, however, typically limit student's reflection and focus more on a re-stating and re-writing of the major ideas and themes within a book. For seasoned teachers, this assignment can be especially painful to grade, as they encounter reports on the same books year after year. Book reports are not the only way for students to show their knowledge and comprehension of a particular book. Many times there are far better options. Teachers can provide students with a variety of choices, including:

- Book reviews (similar to those in newspapers and magazines).
- Letters to characters.
- Letters to the author.
- Abstracts of the text (for non-fiction text) written for a particular audience.
- Transformation of part of the book to another genre (e.g. poem, short story, video).
- Artistic representation of the text (e.g. artistic responses such as the design of a poster or book jacket).
- Role-playing scenes.
- Speech or presentation.

All of these book report alternatives can require students to refine their understanding of the text. Quotes and significant details can be extracted from the text and organized into a meaningful piece of writing. In the process of participating in these activities, students' understanding of and reflection on the text is both enriched and displayed.

Summer reading can also be related directly to the curriculum. Though some schools simply ask students to read a certain number of books, without placing limitations on content, summer reading can also be used to frontload themes and ideas central to the class and to give students the opportunity to preview some of the topics that they'll be exploring in the new school year. In this scenario, teachers and schools can allow students to make selections among a limited set of options that connect directly to the first unit of study in the fall. This maintains some aspect of choice among the students while also providing teachers with a way to exert a certain degree of control over the content. It is best, especially at the middle and high school level, if the book choices represent a variety of styles, genres and topics as well. This is an effective way to blend choice and reading for pleasure with the requirements of a structured curriculum. In September, teachers can begin class by organizing students who have chosen the same texts into small groups for discussions and projects. These groups can meet and then share their responses with the whole class individually or collectively. Only after those discussions and conversations take place should assessments occur - not as an immediate 'gotcha', but as a follow-up to the discussion and writing.

Subsequently, the first novel or text that is read during the first unit of study can be compared and contrasted with the students' summer reading. Students can also act as consultants to the summer reading program by reviewing books under consideration for the summer reading selection. Teachers can also collect data about students' responses to particular books and use the information to help the next grade of students in selecting their own choices from the list. Additionally, student assignments could include 'selling' the summer reading books that they've chosen and read to the students in the grade or grades below them. Students can post reviews online in a blog, create posters and infographics about their selected book, or prepare a video or podcast to share their opinions.

Book Talks

Book talks are also a great way for students to be introduced to different books and types of texts. In a book talk, students are invited to share what they are reading or a book that they have already read and enjoyed. A book talk can be done in small groups or with a whole class share, and is done mostly by volunteers. Teachers can also participate in book talks and can invite others from within the school or community to share books with the students in their class. Not surprisingly, many students will be inspired to read the books that are shared during a book talk, and can also encourage students to participate more in the book talks once they understand the role and structure (or unstructured) organization of the process. Depending on the age of the students, they can also use an Author's Chair or Book Talk Chair to discuss and share the books they are reading.

Reading During Class

Historically, teachers have been hesitant to allow students to read during class time. Teaching is categorized as an activity. Often, when an administrator enters the classroom, there is an assumption that the teacher should be actively teaching and the students should be receptively learning. Though it may not appear to be an active lesson, when students read in the classroom they are engaging in active learning, processing and transacting. Despite the myth of what "active teaching" and "active learning" look like, teachers should not be afraid to allow reading during class time—at any level.

Many adolescents stop reading for pleasure when they transition into departmentalized schedules during the school day. This often occurs in fifth or sixth grade. It also drops off considerably when school assignments become more demanding, which is typically around seventh grade. When teachers provide students with the time to engage in self-initiated and self-selected independent reading — often paired with writing— they support students getting the message that extensive reading is important and critical to their learning — that it is not just an enrichment activity or something that should be limited to certain classes or specific students.

An Example of Extending Reading in a School Setting

Penn Manor High School in Millersville, Pennsylvania began a school-wide reading initiative in 2005 that supported extending reading and writing in all areas of the school. The school administration and staff engaged all students in school-wide Friday reading for the first fifteen minutes in every 90 minute block across the curriculum. Students and teachers alike were asked to pick a text to read; it could be a novel, magazine, newspaper or something else. Students not only actively participated in the reading, but the reading became a part of the fabric of the school community. It changed the way that teachers interacted with students and literally changed the landscape of the school. More students began carrying books with them, pulling them out to read when they had time. There was a general consensus among the faculty that students read more often when they completed an assignment or test early. They read between classes, and teachers read with them. It was an amazing result from a concentrated effort to get kids reading more and more. This might look different in a school that does not have a block schedule. The goal of reading for one hour during the school day can be organized in a variety of ways that fits into the current school schedule.

A Final Word

Extending Reading and Writing focuses on providing a classroom structure in which students can exercise significant choice and control over their own learning and engagement with reading and writing. To accomplish this goal, self-selected sustained reading, writing and book sharing should be integrated into the entire curriculum and encouraged at home. While it is useful to supplement existing curriculum, it can also be a critical part of the curriculum.

Chapter 8
Process 4: Investigating Language

Through sentence making and word making, composing and reading would be more directly related to a learner's spoken language. As they compose in this way they are exploring the systems that govern written English.

James Britton

The first three of The Five Reading, Writing, and Talking Processes focus on using language. They focus students' attention on co-constructing ideas throughout the curriculum using the interrelated language tools of listening, speaking, and reading and writing. When teachers guide students to use these methods to learn about literature, history, science, math, and other topics, language is mainly a transparent process. Students are engaged in their learning, and find real world meaning with little conscious awareness of the way that language is organized, formed and utilized through the text. At the same time that they are using language to learn about the world, students are developing considerable proficiency with the content in their speech and writing. Thus, students who read and write a lot not only learn about ideas, but also about language and its usage.

Investigating Language focuses on introducing students to linguistic structure and language conventions in a more explicit manner. This learning should take place through language investigations in which they experience language as a process, not simply as a product or vehicle for knowledge. As they engage with reading and experiment with writing, students simultaneously see, talk about, manipulate and become aware of language elements and patterns. When the teacher focuses on instructing students through guided studies of various language processes and structures, students become even more directly aware of the language itself. They can use their growing awareness to decode and spell words, to learn specific vocabulary, to speak and write in sentences, and to develop insights into the uses of language. This is known as 'intuitive grammar' and contrasts with the more abstract study of 'formal grammar'. The metalinguistic understandings of language incorporate students' understanding of the meaning of words, syntactic context, as well as phonological and phonemic awareness.

An Uneven Playing Field

Vocabulary is one of the most critical aspects of a student's reading capability, as the wider a student's vocabulary is, the more he or she is able to understand from reading. Students who know more words are better able to interact with the text, to bring more background knowledge to their reading, and to co-construct meaning without struggling to determine what is actually being communicated. Words are the building blocks of reading; helping each student to build structures to support his or her understanding of text and the world. When a student has a wider vocabulary, the structures they build can be higher and sturdier. Students with more expansive vocabularies simply read more ably than those with limited vocabularies. Vocabulary acquisition begins well before students enter school, or even pre-school. Children are exposed to words from birth, and their interaction with parents and caregivers play a huge role in the amount of language and the type of language that they experience.

A study conducted by the National Institute of Health in 1999 indicated that students' vocabulary, when they enter kindergarten, has a direct correlation to their socio-economic level. They reported that children from families at or below the poverty line hear 600-700 words per hour between the ages of 12 and 18 months, and by the time these same children enter kindergarten they will have vocabularies of approximately 5000 words. By contrast, children from middle-income families hear between 1200 and 1300 words per hour between 12 and 18 months of age, and by the time they enter kindergarten they will have vocabularies of approximately 9000 words. Children from upper-income families hear between 2900 and 3100 words per hour between 12 and 18 months of age, and by the time they enter kindergarten they have vocabularies of approximately 15,000 to 20,000 words. (NIH, 1999)

These results are staggering, and are another indication that the educational playing field is not level for all children. As students progress through school, these achievement gaps tend to remain wide and become even wider. Teachers face an uphill battle as they try to expand students' understanding of text as they read, write, speak and listen to their peers in discrete, meaningful ways. The critical role that vocabulary plays in student learning is compounded by this gap, and many times students do not yet know the words that teachers think they should already have learned; thus the gap widens further. For example, a teacher in a ninth grade English class noted her surprise when a student did not know the word 'wise'. This experience made her question the weekly vocabulary lists that she prepared. She wondered what other words were missing from her students' vocabularies. There is no easy solution to this problem, and in many ways the focus is misplaced on schools, as this learning begins at birth. Regardless of the gaps, teachers need to creatively and meaningfully teach students in a way that helps them to acquire vocabularies and personal lexicons that can assist them in their education, and allow them to co-construct text in meaningful ways.

The Process of Language

Investigating Language focuses on how students can learn about language while speaking, listening, reading and writing in school. Regardless of the expansiveness of their own personal lexicon, children come to school with a broad knowledge of language, both in words and word usage. They have strong intuitions about the nature and function of language beyond what they already know. Native speakers of any language know what sounds right or does not fit, even if they do not know the official grammar rule that is behind it. Many students can readily identify sentences that make sense and distinguish them from sentences that do not, even if they cannot immediately describe the patterns or reasons why they might be right or wrong. In this way, students are demonstrating their ability to use language rules rather than just to state them. Though the nuances of grammar and correct word usage can be challenging for students Pre-K-12, most students can determine if a sentence makes sense or if it is complete nonsense. Teachers can start from this basic ability and build upon it to work toward a more sophisticated knowledge of language patterns and linguistic diversity. The teacher's role is to clarify, refine, and help learners to extend what they already know, and expand and elaborate on the language learning that is already occurring.

Most textbooks and workbooks are based on the assumption that language is best learned in a pre-determined sequence. Students who successfully complete these activities are presumed to have mastered particular skills in isolation that can then transfer into competence in 'real' reading, writing and speaking. Instruction and activities that teach vocabulary in isolation do not work to improve grammatical skillfulness. Continued work on the writing process and investigating the language processes in the context of the learning that is already taking place in the class — either through the content or the products of the class — is much more influential in student learning, and allows students to see the role of the content as a part of the language learning process rather than a separate issue that is then layered on top of "actual" learning.

One of the appeals of using vocabulary and grammar workbooks to teach these skills is that they review aspects of these skills in a logical sequence. Instead of relying on supplemental curriculum pieces that are unrelated to any content from the curriculum, teachers can create lessons that systematically incorporate these language lessons within the context of the content and language being used in the class. Teachers can also use students' own writing to teach vocabulary and grammar in mini-lessons and classroom investigations.

While learning about literature, science, math or history, students can also be encouraged to ask their own questions about language: "Who is my audience?" "How can I signal different sections of my writing?" "How do I explain when things occurred?" "Why does the author use this word?" "How does this idea relate to that one?" "What are some good opening lines?" "How can I conclude this in a meaningful way?" These questions help students to shift their attention to the language and word choice and/or grammar choices that they make within the context of their own writing. Even paying brief attention to their language enhances students' metalinguistic awareness; helping them become more aware about the ways language is systematic and patterned. This allows them to see how their own choices compare to other texts, their spoken language, and their peers' choices.

Vocabulary Investigations

Vocabulary is one aspect of Investigating Language through which teachers aim to expand student knowledge of words, increase their comprehension of oral and written language, and encourage students to develop strategies for learning words independently. It also benefits students when they are interested in words, curious about where they came from and how they might be used, and motivated to use them in their subsequent writing. If students want to learn how to express themselves coherently and precisely, learning vocabulary is the key to their own self-expression, and central to their ability to communicate effectively. There are many ways to view vocabulary acquisition, and a variety of ways that teachers in all content areas can support students in learning vocabulary for their own particular content, as well as in relation to the larger goal of expanding vocabulary in all content areas.

In many classrooms, vocabulary is a separate subject, complete with its own materials and routines. Teachers provide words and definitions, instruct students in creating sentences or completing exercises, and eventually test them on their learning. This time-consuming process yields mixed results at best. Students may 'learn' words - or provide correct answers on tests and quizzes — but do not actually use them in their speaking or writing. The memorization that this type of vocabulary interaction produces does not typically equate to actual learning or vocabulary integration with a student's own lexicon. Many students who simply memorize words do not acquire interest in them, or the curiosity about vocabulary that leads to effective and independent lifetime learning strategies.

Students learn vocabulary and experience vocabulary growth from extensive reading. Students who are avid readers acquire knowledge about language quickly and easily, without much effort on the part of either the student or the teacher.

In order to best support students in acquiring vast and varied vocabularies, teachers need to facilitate vocabulary instruction both directly and indirectly — through the content they provide as a direct part of the curriculum and also as a result of directed study and investigations. There is no one right way to teach and learn vocabulary. Teachers should incorporate a variety of strategies and methods to help students interact with words to support their learning across the curriculum. The following suggestions are not all-inclusive for instruction. However, they are springboards for implementing vocabulary-involved investigations that focus on integrating vocabulary instruction into whatever content area learning is already taking place. These approaches introduce vocabulary and the teaching of words in all aspects of language – listening, speaking, reading and writing. Each of these strategies can be adapted to fit different grade levels and content areas across the curriculum.

Self-Selected Vocabulary Words

Teachers are encouraged to have students to create their own vocabulary lists from the words in their reading, as well as from their interactions in class. This strategy does not replace teacher-selected words, but does provide an opportunity for choice to the class vocabulary lists. Students can be encouraged to choose words they think other students in the class should learn too. This might result in a class word list. Students who are able to choose their own words can then focus on ones that are important to words that are important to them and at their own reading level. These self-selected lists can be shared with partners, displayed on a class word wall, or incorporated into both formative and summative assessments.

Vocabulary Building

A great way to introduce new vocabulary and informally assess students' knowledge of specific words is to ask them to chart a list of words that appear in their text from 'New' to 'Known' (see below for a chart to use with students). Ask students to place the words on the chart depending on how well they know the word, and then use their classmates to help them understand what a word means. Once the students have discussed the vocabulary in small groups, they can use context clues to help them learn the words that they still do not know and move them into the 'Recognized' or 'Known' area. Brainstorming, mapping, and spontaneous writing can help to stimulate students' prior knowledge and associations with a "new" word encountered in reading, discussion or other media.

Example of a handout for Vocabulary Building:

Vocabulary Building: *New* to *Known*!		
New *Words that you have never seen before:*	**Recognized** *Words that you think you know, but you're not sure:*	**Known** *Words that you know well and can use in a sentence:*

Word Play

Robert Marzano advocates playing with words in his book *Vocabulary Games for the Classroom* (2010), and states that students should be encouraged to play with words using puns, riddles, puzzles, and cartoons or to create their own vocabulary and word games. The more students interact with the words they are learning, the more they can internalize the meanings of these words and allow them to become part of their own vocabulary.

Mapping Words

Teachers can encourage students to think about the many meanings and connections that they have to words by allowing them to map the words, or create concept maps of the ideas surrounding each word.

Students can then share their maps and discuss how they connected their words and ideas, and also compare how different student groups made connections of their own. With young children, this can be structured as a whole class activity, and students can be encouraged to draw their words and make connections as well.

Selecting Vocabulary Words

Selecting vocabulary words can be done on a grade level or teacher level, depending on the school. If teachers are able to select vocabulary words for their own classes, it can be important to select words in a strategic and meaningful way. One way to do this is to select one or two concept words and use brainstorming, mapping and writing before reading a text so that students can access their own prior knowledge of the words and concepts. Students can work in pairs to discuss how three or five words might be used in the text, what they expect the topic of the text will be, and/or the questions they expect the text to answer.

When at all possible, it's important that teachers select vocabulary words that are related to one another. These connected words can help students make connections among the words on their list and allow them to see the semantic relationships as well. Students may find that they have connections or familiarity with words that they did not expect. Knowing a word can mean many things to students. They may never have seen a word before, but have an intuitive understanding of it, or students may have seen the word before and be able to approximate its meaning. They may be able to attach meaning to a word with or without actually knowing the true definition of a word, or it may be an established part of their reading, writing, and speaking. All of these represent different degrees of knowing a word and students who can play with the words, or spend time investigating the vocabulary can help students make those connections.

Grammar and Language Investigations

When people use the word *grammar* they may mean a number of different things. It may be intended to mean correct grammar — what is taught in school as language rules. Many of these rules sound more like commands: "Do not write a sentence fragment," or "Never end a sentence with a preposition," or "Do not split an infinitive." These rules are often vague and abstract, and there are many exceptions given the realities of written language. Learning these language guidelines can be very challenging, and make it difficult to grasp all of the nuances associated with language and the differences in rules for written and spoken language.

These commands and grammar rules attempt to smooth over fundamental and persistent problems in grammar instruction. Frequently, there is an overemphasis on individual parts of speech and language. Despite this focus, students often fail to remember grammar rules from year to year despite regular instruction. Explicitly teaching grammar rules does not improve writing, nor does it improve speaking. Grammar workbooks and drills can be very time consuming, and take time away from the class content. In a middle school English classroom, one day spent on grammar, another spent on vocabulary, and a third day to test leaves little time for authentic reading and writing.

Grammar and language rules – re-conceptualized as grammatical discourse and sociolinguistic competence – can and should be infused into classroom instruction wherever possible. Students need to be supported in understanding how their language **works** and in acquiring metalinguistic awareness through activities that enhance the awareness of language as language, not by focusing on categories or labels. Grammatical competence can be developed in relation to students' own writing using activities like the ones suggested below. These involve "doing' grammar rather than learning from rules and exercises.

Keep Records of Difficult Structures:

Teachers can keep an informal record of each student's strengths and weaknesses with writing. These could be sentence fragments, shifting verb tense, difficulty with plurals and possessives, agreement, and punctuation, among others. The student record can also include stylistic and organizational aspects, and broader concerns related to effective writing in different genres and for different purposes. Teachers can consider keeping this record with students' Writer's Workshop notes.

Mini-lessons of Challenging Rules:

When a number of students are having a similar difficulty, teachers can engage the class in a five- or ten-minute mini-lesson on the concept, using examples from the students' own writing or examples from a language book. Teachers can use a problem-solving format, asking students to work together to look at an incorrect sentence or phrase and then focus on the challenging area. After looking at the particular parts of the sentence or phrase, put the text back together so that students can see the bigger picture of the grammar rule. This approach may take longer, but it pays off in student interest and retention.

Teachers can also provide students with one or two corrected examples of common grammatical issues on a poster or shared folder for student reference.

Peer Editing Groups:

Teachers can set up peer editing activities where students are responsible for noticing the concepts that have been taught in mini lessons, or have been emphasized in class. Encourage students to add to this list, identifying patterns they think are important and valuable for the whole class.

A Spiral Grammar Curriculum

The underlying premise in The Five Reading, Writing & Talking Processes is that students do not actually master processes, but rather— if carefully coached — they become increasingly competent in using these processes to learn about ideas across the curriculum. This is the essential nature of a spiral curriculum. Indeed, most skills and strategies should be taught and re-taught at each grade level at higher levels of sophistication.

The processes of investigating sentences and words are also spiral in nature since at every level they involve students in investigations where they arrange and rearrange words and letters to make sentences and words. By doing so, they get better at manipulating elements and, through that practice, at discovering patterns, decoding and spelling, speaking, and writing standard English sentences.

Teachers, literacy theorists and researchers alike recognize the importance of continuing to help students learn about language informally, experientially and implicitly. They believe that students become skillful in decoding through the processes of self-selected reading, composing and teacher-facilitated reading for meaning. In addition to the intuitive knowledge gained when learning about the world, teachers use these processes to take advantage of teachable moments, and also to develop mini lessons to strengthen students' skills. The main purpose conducting explicit linguistic investigations with students is to further extend that knowledge and skillfulness.

The proposal that follows may be called The Third Way. Approaches to teaching decoding generally fall into two camps: advocates of holistic language teaching and advocates of a phonics first approach. Holistic teaching advocates typically favor the learning of language as language, and do not support breaking language down words into fragmented pieces for learning. The supporters of holistic language teaching generally advocate that teachers use teachable moments to focus on grammar and language issues when students need help. Phonics advocates follow a hierarchical model of learning to read, and support breaking words down into manageable pieces for students to learn to recognize commonalities in words, language, and similarities in words across language. These two approaches come from opposite ends of the spectrum, and there are many variations that can be found in between.

The Third Way was advocated by James Moffett and Betty Jane Wagner. In their article What Works Is Play, they make significant observations about the importance of students playing with parts of words as important intellectual and integrative experiences:

With Regard to Inventive Spelling

> *To the extent that beginning writers use words they do not already know how to spell, they will have to rely on some knowledge of phoneme spellings going well beyond the alphabet. Starting with the sound of their own words*

136

in their minds, writers must build up phoneme by phoneme each word that they haven't memorized the spelling of...

Inventing spelling is the same kind of creative, intellectual play that makes small children the prodigious learners they are. Letters are a new play medium, the alphabet a generative toy whose possibilities they play out by combining members of the set to learn which combinations can stand for sounds and words they want...

In other words, the learning of isolated letters or letter clusters that do not appear holistic from the perspective of language communication alone appear integrative from the learner's perspective, wherein letters, phonemes, and words are play tokens (parts as representing wholes) as well as symbols. Knowing that putting them together can also tie into meaning does not in the child's mind conflict with this but rather enhances it.

With Regard to Word-Making Games

Most games depend on social interplay. Players pool their knowledge. Game materials... provide the sight, or spellings, but players have to provide the sound or oral language. Collectively, they have enough knowledge of word recognition and sound-spellings to play the game, but while one player may only be practicing a sound spelling or a word she already knows, another player in the game may be learning the sound spelling or word for the first time.

Moffett and Wagner find the "play" of invented spelling and word-making games powerful processes for going from parts of words to whole words (called analysis through synthesis by cognitive psychologists). In a reciprocal process, students are learning to spell and decode and, in that process, to develop phonological and phonemic awareness.

Sentence-making, sentence-combining and word-making games enable students to play and explore by manipulating word and sentence elements to create many words and sentences. While playing the games, they talk with their partners and make discoveries about oral and written sentence and word patterns and structures. These game-like, problem-solving activities provide experiences that 'perplex' and challenge students' minds and are a valuable replacement for learning rote phonics and sentence rules.

Students benefit when they experience explicit sentence-level investigations in conjunction with word-making investigations. In creating the investigations and fostering an environment that supports these investigations, the goals of these investigations need to be broad enough to gain control of the conventions of oral and written English including its usage, capitalization and punctuation, as well as of the graphophonic system. Additionally, structural analysis or skillfulness in identifying printed words that are made up of root words and affixes (like want/wants/wanting/wanted) or contrasting forms of pronouns (like she/her) are understood best in the context of sentences.

Investigating Language is a process that helps to develop students' skillfulness in decoding, spelling and the conventions of oral and written language. This way of teaching grammar and language structures draws from the implicit learning that takes place in the context of the reading and writing processes, and also advocates students' investigations of the grammatical and graphophonic systems through sentence-making, sentence-combining and word-making.

Through carefully developed word-making, sentence-making and sentence-combining games, students continue to increase their metalinguistic awareness and skillfulness in the specific aspects of sentences listed on pages 144-147. This listing, and subsequent word and sentence listings on pages 144-147 might be thought of as a short, informal summary of the formal structure of language.

Through word-making games, students will continue to increase their phonological, phonemic and graphophonic awareness and skillfulness in the eight major spelling pattern clusters on page 144-147. These explanations are meant to provide a review of knowledge that most teachers already have, and to provide a foundation for the manipulative activities with sentences and words that teachers create.

Sentence-Combining Investigations:

(Note: Teachers who may not be familiar with research-based sentence-combining investigations can see the appendix for more elaboration of those activities.)

Students can experiment with Sentence-Combining Investigations with content derived both from literature and from their own writing. This focuses students' attention explicitly on investigating the syntactic organization of language and the unlimited ways that words can be combined into sentences and sentences combined, expanded or elaborated to produce new sentences. Sentencing activities are most useful as a component of revision and can be used to help students see how to make their sentences more effective and deconstruct sentences that are too complex.

The main purpose of having students play Sentence-Combining Games is that students will become more competent using the conventions of language in their own writing. It is important that these experiences be separated from the writing program. As Jerome Bruner emphasized, students learn subjects best by doing— in this case "doing grammar". Through the processes of learning, such as Sentence-Combining Investigations, students become more aware of the processes and regularities of

language. This approach is also inspired by the theory of "transformational grammar" and the research of John Mellon.

There are two types of Sentence-Combining Investigations: Composing & Decomposing Sentences.

Composing: How many ways can you combine two or three related sentences?

Example: The lion roared. The lion was hungry. She was mad. Students might come up with the following possible combined sentences in these investigation:

- The lion roared because she was mad and hungry.
- Because the hungry lion was mad, she roared.
- The mad lion that roared was hungry.
- The hungry lion that roared was mad.

Decomposing: How many simple sentences can be derived from a complicated sentence?

In these investigations the teacher rewrites a paragraph or two of a story in simple sentences. For example:

> *When the hunter walked into town the citizens stood by and watched. The men, women and children stared; their eyes wide open with surprise.*

The teacher then rewrites the paragraph into simple sentences:

The hunter walked into town. The citizens stood by. They watched. The men stared. The women stared. The children stared. Their eyes were wide open with surprise.

After teachers introduce these investigations, students can work on their own composing and decomposing investigations in pairs, triads even as a form of assessment.

Sentence-Making Games

Sentence-making games allow students to experiment with words and phrasing in a playful and experiential way. They foster a sense of inquiry and interest in language and words, and shows them the varying ways to express themselves through the structure of their sentences. There are many ways to support sentence-making games.

How Many?

How Many is a great sentence-making game that the teacher can organize by posting two or three words for the class, and allowing the students to create as many sentences as they can using the posted words (and any helper words that the teacher wants to allow: the, and, am, a, with, to, etc.) Teachers can start by using only one word on each card, and then expanding to at least two cards and then three. Students should be encouraged to capitalize and punctuate the sentences as they write them down. In the case of a first game, the words that a teacher selects may be "play, me and cat". Some of the many possible sentences are:

I play.	The cats play with me.
The cat plays.	Play with me.
The cats play.	Play with me?
I play with the cat.	Play with the cat.
I play with the cats.	Play with the cats.
The cat plays with me.	

Another sentence-making game can include six cards — the original ones and two more: to and want, wants. Many additional possible sentences can be made. Teachers can then add cards as desired, including additional helper words, the "ing" ending, and other elements that can encourage further exploration. Including various forms of a verb on the cards can create more complex sentences such as: make, makes, making, made; more forms of the "be" verb: is, am, was, and were. Other possibilities include allowing one card to be a "wild card" which can be any word students choose.

Found Poetry

In middle and high school settings, these word-making games can focus on content as well as skills, and support students in making connections between seemingly random words from a text. In this way, teachers can provide students with slips of paper with many vocabulary words, and ask them to create as many sentences as **they** can using the vocabulary words, possibly asking for a minimum of 3 words in each sentence.

Word-Making Games

In word-making games, students are simultaneously learning the letters of the alphabet, phonological awareness, and phonemic awareness, as well as graphophonic awareness — all within the framework of the syllable.

Singing the Vowel: A powerful approach to learning phonics

Occasionally, consider engaging students in **Singing the Vowel** exercises before, or instead of word-making activities. The concept behind this activity is rooted in the understanding that except for a few letters (s, f, th, sh for example) letters cannot be extended without adding a vowel sound. So when a teacher tells a child to sound out a letter or word like bat, you get *buh-ah-tuh*. Research in psychoacoustics, as reported by Gleitman and Rozin, has shown that such exercises are difficult for students to process, especially those who have trouble learning to read. Extending the vowel sound alleviates some of the difficulty and minimizes word distortion.

For example, when teachers investigate the Consonant Vowel Consonant (CVC) Pattern they can display one word, **bat**, from that pattern. The teacher can sing the whole word, but extend the vowel sound to: *baaaaaat*. Have the students sing *baaaaaat* with you noting the *aaaaaa* extended. Then, cover the b and sing the rest of the syllable: *aaaaaat*. Then, cover the t and sing the rest of the syllable: *baaaaaa*. Then erase the b and t and sing the rest of the syllable: *aaaaaa*. This experience is a powerful way to develop students' phonological awareness, phonemic awareness, and phonics in a research-proven and articulated way, and reminds students not to say *buh-ah-tuh*.

Playing Sentence- and Word-Making Games

Teachers can make the games individually, but when teachers can work together their collaboration frequently enhances the activities that they create. This can also offer a sense of community, aid in grade level strategic planning and provide more opportunities for teachers to communicate and discuss their teaching and content, which is always valuable.

Language Study Across The Curriculum

Students' awareness of language in use — their "sociolinguistic competence" — can be enhanced by establishing opportunities for them to gather examples of how language is used in many settings including school, home, community, experiences and books or other types of text. These topics for investigation are appropriate across the curriculum, and are best taught when integrated with thematic or topical units.

Examples include:

Dialects	Computer Languages	Semantics
Metaphor	Slang/Jargon	Censorship And Taboo
Language And Politics	Propaganda/Doublespeak	Nonverbal Communication
Language And Gender	The Language Of Sports	The Language Of The Media
Word Play	Etymology	Euphemisms
Language Attitudes	Codes And Ciphers	Language Acquisition
Roots And Affixes	Humor	

A Final Word

The teaching of conventional grammar, with its emphasis on isolated drills, does not contribute to the ability of students to write or use grammar effectively. There is considerable research supporting the fact that language skills are enhanced through authentic writing and from independent investigation patterns and features of language. Activities that center on word meanings and sentence structures are a natural part of co-constructing text. To supplement these activities, teachers can engage students in research-based sentence-making, sentence-combining and word-making games, and vocabulary and grammar investigations. Through these investigations students will enhance their metalinguistic awareness of the structural meanings in language by combining, subtracting, substituting, arranging and rearranging the elements of language into words, sentences and linguistic patterns. While investigating, students talk with partners and classmates about their constructions and the patterns found, thus providing them with rich opportunities to connect corresponding visual and auditory forms.

Appendix to Chapter 8:

Sentence and Word Investigations

With the following resources, teachers can create their own classroom investigations with Standard English sentences.

The Relationship between Simple and Compound/Complex Sentences

Six patterns of simple sentences account for most common simple sentences in English:

> **1. NP+VP:** The dog barks.
> **2. NP+VP+NP:** Mr. Jones honked the horn.
> **3. NP+be verb+NP:** They are friends.
> **4. NP+be verb+Adjective:** She is lovely.
> **5. NP+be verb+Adverb:** We are alone.
> **6. NP+VP+NP+NP:** The librarian gave me the book.

> NP: Noun Phrase
> VP: Verb Phrase

Simple sentences are still regarded as "simple" when they are transformed into questions, exclamations and imperatives. Thus, in the first sentence pattern: *Does the dog bark?* falls in the same category as *The dog is barking!* The second sentence pattern: Bring the groceries! In these sentences the Noun Phrase (you) is understood.

Additionally, there are six systematic high-frequency Sentence-Combining Processes:

> 1. **Use Coordinating Conjunctions**: and, but, for, or, so, yet
>   Combined Sentence: Mr. Jones honked the horn and the dog barked.
>   Sentences Combined: Mr. Jones honked. The dog barked.
>
> 2. **Use Subordinating Conjunctions**: after, although, if, since, when
>   Combined Sentence: After Mr. Jones honked the horn, the dog barked.
>   Sentences Combined: Mr. Jones honked. The dog barked.

3. **Combining a Series with "and":**
   Combined Sentence: Mr. Jones, Mrs. Jones and I talked to the dog.
   Sentences Combined: Mr. Jones talked to the dog. Mrs. Jones talked to the dog. I talked to the dog.

4. **Using Relative Clauses**: who-whom, and that
   Combined Sentence: Mr. Jones looked at the dog that barked.
   Sentences combined: Mr. Jones looked at the dog. The dog barked.

5. **Using Appositives:**
   Combined Sentence: Mr. Jones, my neighbor, looked at the dog.
   Sentences Combined: Mr. Jones looked at the dog. Mr. Jones is my neighbor.

6. **Using the Verb Ending "ing":**
   Combined Sentence: Mr. Jones looked at the barking dog.
   Sentence Combined: Mr. Jones looked at the dog. The dog was barking.

Metalinguistic Awareness of the System of Sentence Processes

While playing sentence-making and sentence-combining games, students gain increasing metalinguistic awareness of, and control of, the following main conventions of Standard English:

1. The concept of standard and non-standard: People speak in different ways at different times and for different purposes. Students learn the value of the language of his or her home and community and, at the same time, learn to use Standard English, which can be more effective in writing, specifically.

2. **Sentence sense**: The intonation patterns or sounds of complete sentences.

3. **The functional parts of a sentence:** The noun phrase as subject or object (The boy loves the dog). The verb phrase as a verb or as a verb plus a complement (The boys are walking. The boys are walking the dog.) Pronouns as substituted for noun phrases (They are walking.) Adverbs as additions to sentences (They are walking fast.)

4. **The nature of grammatical categories in a sentence:** Different words can be substituted in the same slot in a sentence (The boy chases the dog. The dog chases the boy. The boy loves the dog.)

5. **The nature of nouns:** The forms and functions that make nouns a special class of words in English. Nouns can be subjects or objects (boy-boys, fox-foxes, girl-girls).

6. **The nature of verbs:** The forms and functions that make verbs a special class of words in English (the "be" verb forms: be-am-is-are-was etc., regular verb forms: play-plays-played-playing, irregular verb forms: run-runs-ran-running).

7. **The –s form of verbs:** Choosing the –s form of the verb in the present tense when the subject is third person singular and, conversely, of choosing the uninflected verb form for other subjects (He runs. *versus* You run. The girls run.)

8. **Compound noun phrases:** Parts of sentences can be added by the use of the word "and".

9. **The nature of pronouns:** Using the correct forms of pronouns according to their function (subject or object) in a sentence (Tom and I ran. *versus* Tom and me ran) and that pronouns substitute for noun phrases (They ran.)

10. **The nature of adverbs:** The ability of adverbs to function in different positions in a sentence (They ran away. Away they ran.)

11. **The function of helping verbs:** Using special helping verbs (be, have, and the modals: will-would, can-could) that are added before main verbs (He is walking. They are walking. They have gone away. They will come here.)

Metalinguistic Awareness of the System of Graphophonic Processes

It is beneficial for students to play these games on a regular basis. When they play the word-making games, students investigate the graphophonic patterns below. Students will learn the other structures from reading in context and exploration. In all cases below, the C represents one or two consonants while V represents one vowel.

1. **Consonant + rime**: Words or names in the "onset and rime" pattern, (often referred to as initial consonant(s) and rhyming element), such as bat/cat/fat/ hat/mat/pat.

2. **The CVC pattern**: Words that have the regularly spelled CVC (short vowel) pattern (C= consonant or consonant digraph, V= vowel), such as: fan, hop, met.

3. **The CVCe pattern**: Words that have the regularly spelled CVCe (where the final 'e' signals a long vowel sound) pattern such as: make, Pete, prize, home, tube.

4. **The CeeC and CeaC patterns**: Words that have the semi-regularly spelled long "e" vowel sound patterns CeeC such as feet, sleep, tree and CeaC such as eat, clear, tea.

5. **The Cay and CaiC patterns**: Words that have the semi-regularly spelled long "a" vowel sound patterns Cay such as play, day, may, and CaiC such as train, paint, rain.

6. **The CoaC and CowC patterns:** Words that have the semi-regularly spelled long "o" vowel sound patterns such as boat, road, float, and show, shown, own.

7. **The CooC patterns**: Words that have the semi-regularly spelled long and short "oo", vowel sound patterns such as soon, too, school and good, book, brook.

8. **The CVr pattern**: Words that have the semi-regularly spelled "r-controlled" pattern, such as far, farm, start.

Chapter 9
Process 5: Learning to Learn

How do children learn best? Teachers and education experts have many answers to this question, but the most important answer comes from each individual student. Each learners strengths and weaknesses are different, and it is very beneficial for each individual to be able to answer that question for themselves. In this chapter we will explore the different ways that this benefits teachers and students alike, as well as how to develop and investigate strategies to enhance individual discovery.

The fifth Reading Writing and Talking Process focuses on supporting students as they become more reflective and strategic about their own knowledge, purposes, and methods as learners. When teachers and parents shift attention in this direction, it allows students to discover and determine their individual and distinct learning process. Students enable themselves to increase the range and depth of their own independence and interdependence as learners, and to deepen their knowledge, understanding, and ability to create new learning independently.

The goal is to empower students to develop their repertoire of strategies by using oral and written language to learn on their own, in groups, and with teachers, parents, and other adults. Talking and writing about how they learn helps students understand their own knowledge. It also enhances their ability to acquire new facts and concepts, and promotes higher order thinking. Through thinking about learning and engaging in metacognition, students of all ages become increasingly conscious of the strategies they use to learn in different situations. Students determine their own strengths and weaknesses and develop a better understanding of their own processes as learners.

Students' attitudes are central to learning how to learn. Students need to be willing to work hard and to have expectations for their own success. When they have a general inquisitiveness and tolerance for ambiguity, as well as feelings of their own self-worth and ability to learn, they are more open to their own learning, and increasingly able to make sense of how and why they learn the way that they do. The ability to think about their learning and assess it in a meaningful way affects their learning quality both in and out of school.

This metacognition should be woven into the fabric of content and classroom interactions rather than separated into its own subject to master. When students think about their own thinking processes and learning needs in the context of their own curriculum and subject matter content, it provides an enhancement of each of the other Reading, Writing and Talking Processes.

The importance of metacognition seems self-evident. To become most effective, learners need a solid repertoire of flexible — albeit not always conscious — strategies for reading and writing different texts for different purposes.

Although individuals implement strategies such as note making, questioning and collaborating, these are fundamentally social acts learned in social contexts. Unless they are encouraged to analyze or interpret what they read, young readers are likely to take the text as a given, reading opinions as if they were facts. Even if teachers ask for interpretations, students do not automatically know what strategies are appropriate or how to use them when working on their own. Simply answering teachers' interpretative questions does not teach students to interpret, nor does the suggestion to 'preview' or 'survey' a text before reading mean that students will know why or how to use those strategies. Weaving metacognitive instruction into the overall curriculum is the comprehensive and long-range method to achieve this goal.

Learning-to-learn strategies

Metacognitive strategies are best acquired through engagement with meaningful content, and the classroom activities described in the first four Reading, Writing and Talking Processes include many ways that teachers can help students become more reflective and strategic. Below are seven fundamental activities of learning to learn, applicable Pre-K-12 and across the curriculum. The last is "studying" – doing homework and preparing for tests and examinations – and it requires a synthesis of all the other strategies.

Strategy 1: Questioning

When students come to school, they arrive filled with curiosity. They are active processors of knowledge, naturally motivated to learn and they ask good questions. Research comparing student's questions in and out of school, however, suggests that curiosity questioning, like "Where does gravity come from?" is not often encouraged. The majority of teachers' questions, particularly those requesting specific, right answers, or questions that check comprehension, may leave little time and space for students to become expert questioners, to learn how to investigate subjects of interest, to read to answer their own questions, and to interrogate their own writing in order to improve. Beyond providing a safe climate where they feel free to say "I don't know," teachers at all grade levels can provide regular opportunities for them to self-question and ask questions of their peers and teachers. Teachers can provide instruction on question types and functions, and to design special activities that emphasize questioning.

There are many opportunities for students to question themselves and their own learning, and to generate questions about what they are learning on a daily basis through reading, writing, speaking and listening in the classroom. Before, during and after reading, students can jot down questions about titles, first paragraphs or key terms and ideas from texts, or statements of opinion about the topic being studied. During reading, they can skim texts and pose questions in their margins or on sticky notes. They can be encouraged to question themselves during reading with questions like:

- What stands out for me?
- How do I feel about this?
- Does this make sense?
- What does this text make me think of?
- How does this fit with what I already know?
- What might be added here? Omitted? Changed?
- Where can I apply these ideas?
- What do I agree or disagree with?
- What's not clear here?

Many activities that teachers create heighten students' awareness of the role of questioning, and provide opportunities to raise questions. When students create their own questionnaires, conduct interviews, and are interviewed by a peer, it allows them to focus on creating and recognizing good questions. Additionally, these types of activities introduce students to the concept of clarity in their questions, the number of questions they should ask and the order in which students should ask them. As students focus their own studies in a research or I-Search experience, they can also begin by asking questions and focusing their research as they learn more. In the middle school and beyond, students can make up their own tests and quizzes, which also reinforces the importance of questioning and test-taking skills simultaneously, and helps students to become more aware of important distinctions in test questions and the discrete language that impacts the questions that are asked. See page 59 for a test or quiz writing activity that supports this idea.

When students answer essay or short answer questions, they may not fully understand what the question is asking. Students benefit greatly from the chance to write their own questions and revise one another's questions prior to taking the test itself. This gives students insider knowledge about how questions are framed and about how to avoid ambiguity in formulating questions and in answering them.

Strategy 2: Note-making

Even young children can "make" their own notes by putting words down on paper to describe what they have seen, heard or read. Note-making (instead of note taking) puts the emphasis on the learner's active selection of what to and what not to write, and is significantly different from copying notes from the board or some other pre-selected source. Making notes can also mean "reading with a pencil in hand" – a process that students can begin to learn in the early grades. Learning to annotate texts is fundamental to school learning and can include developing a set of symbols for marking important ideas, questioning the text and recording those questions, and the ability to highlight or underline selectively. Many times, when students are asked to highlight text, they either highlight all of the text or none of it; neither of which is effective. Students need to be instructed on how they can mark the text to create a tool, and this instruction is best when students have the chance to play with the strategies and develop their own as well. Students also benefit and recognize their own learning processes when they are supported in paraphrasing and summarizing readings and text.

Notes can take many forms, and students can be introduced to different note making techniques appropriate to different situations and content areas. Taking notes from listening is different than taking notes from text-rich presentations on PowerPoint or from an online mode. Double Entry Note Making is a valuable tool for students, and provides a structure for self-reflecting and emphasizing, summarizing and paraphrasing the notes that a student records or creates. This model, can be demonstrated by teachers of young children and used independently and with many variations by middle and high schools. Students at all levels, however, who are unfamiliar with the structure and process, need to be instructed on how best to integrate this structure into their note making, and should be plenty of opportunities to practice and refine their own skills.

There are many opportunities for making notes in the classroom. When students have the chance to practice note-making, they become more skilled, and can easily create and re-create notes with their own annotations, thus helping them to see into their own learning and understanding of the content and processes in their classroom.

Strategy 3: Doubting and Believing

The notion that people can examine ideas from two very different stances – as believers or as doubters – has many applications across the grades and curriculum (Elbow 1987.) When students play the game of "Believing" they try to think of everything in their experience (facts, examples, evidence) which supports an idea or proposition. Then they act as doubters and do the opposite – thinking of non-examples, counter-examples, conflicting or contradicting evidence, and whatever they can find which throws doubt on the idea under consideration. This game can be played through a debate format, or by simply posing a quotation from a text before reading, by offering students a clearly biased interpretation of some event or phenomena, or by spontaneously using a student's theory that is offered as part of a discussion. Even very young children can take an idea and think of reasons to doubt or believe it, and older students can use this activity to discuss, write, and prepare for tests. All students benefit when they search for evidence to support ideas that are contrary to their own beliefs.

Strategy 4: Developing a Reader's Repertoire

Reading is different across all content areas and genres. Students read poetry much differently than they read their math textbook or instructions for a science experiment. Students need to acquire reading strategies for different kinds texts, tasks and contexts. Many students do not make distinctions between types of texts and read everything the same way. Good readers select strategies according to particular purposes and usually make four unconscious decisions regarding their reading:

- Purpose: Why am I reading this? What will I do with what I learn?

- Sequence: Should I preview the whole text first?

- Chunking: How is this structured? Should I read only one part at a time and make notes?

- Speed: How fast or slow should I read?

Many students do not ask these questions at all, and simply dive into their reading without any regard to how they can and should proceed. It is very important that students have time to think about this explicitly in the classroom with the support of the teacher and their peers. Students can begin to ask these questions of themselves with practice. Ultimately, the goal is that all students think about their reading before, during and after they are reading text, and not just in terms of the content, but also about what the goal is for that reading and how they can accomplish it. When students read for pleasure they obviously need a different set of strategies than when they are reading to learn or remember the central ideas, text structure, and significant details over time.

Strategy 5: Developing a Writer's Repertoire

Writing is an important area for metacognition, as it provides many chances for students to see into their own thinking and think through their pencils. Strategies for inventing and revising text can help to generate ideas, including:

- brainstorming alone and others,

- asking questions, either of yourself or of others,

- free writing,

- searching through one's own notebook or writer's journal,

- selecting and comparing quotes from stories, novels or non-fiction texts,

- observing or interviewing,

- writing multiple introductions,

- conducting dialogue with an imaginary audience,

- using discovery procedures that vary from "try this first", and

- using sets of questions to help the writer interrogate the subject and make comparisons.

Conferring with a peer or teacher after using one of the approaches above prepares writers to identify problems or points of dissonance. If students bring their own ideas about what works and doesn't in their writing to their conferences with their teacher during Writer's Workshop, they can take more control over their own writing processes, learn to use the teacher or other students as resources, and build general strategies for shaping writing over time.

Strategy 6: Talking to Learn

Exploratory talk is extremely important for clarifying ideas and linking new ideas to the known, yet much of classroom discourse is illustrated by a teacher question/student answer/teacher reaction cycle, a pattern that is also common in written work. Activities like increasing teacher wait-time during questioning, using more diverse and divergent questions, interrupting a whole group discussion so that pairs can confer about an idea or problem can change the dynamics of class discussions and promote active learning.

Teachers also cannot assume that students know how to work together in constructive ways; they need to be instructed explicitly and through fish bowl observations (where a small group participates and the rest of the class observes and comments on the process.) Talking and listening make implicit thinking processes explicit. Students must also learn how to observe and evaluate their own behavior in a group. In order for them to get the most from participating in collaborative learning groups, students need to be taught "talking strategies" – ways to ask and respond to questions, to listen actively to others, to assume various roles in small groups, and to collaborate in problem solving and decision making. Many times, teachers can provide students with sentence or question starters, and models of questions that can be helpful in their small group discussions.

Depending on the needs of the class and class size, teachers can group students according to ability, or randomly in rotating groups so that students can hear from many students, individuals and ideas in their classroom. Many times, teacher-selected groups are best at the beginning of the year, and can increasingly self-select their partners or groups as the class continues with these activities and becomes more comfortable with the expectations.

Strategy 7: Studying

Studying refers to the strategic and metacognitive use of reading, writing and talking to learn from lectures, readings, and taking tests. All students need to be supported in learning how to study. It is important that students learn to see relationships between what they learn in order to create internal systems for managing new information and classifying these systems in their memory. Remembering isolated pieces of information is virtually impossible for long term, meaningful learning. While rote memorization is useful in some instances, it is incompatible with actual learning and cognition, especially for metacognitive purposes. Study skills and learning strategies are often overlooked in teaching, especially in high school when many teachers expect that students have learned this in elementary or middle school. Below are some ways that teachers can support and coach students in different aspects of studying.

Creating Lecture Notes

Guided Lecture Procedure, explained on page 53 provides a structure for involving students in metacognitive strategies while creating notes, and involves listening, writing, reading and re-reading. This method of note-making is most most effective when teachers introduce it to students in the first month or so of the school year. This embeds the guided lecture strategy into the fabric of teaching, and makes it a part of regular instruction in the classroom.

Students usually benefit from direct instruction when first using the Double Entry Note-Making that is utilized in the Guided Lecture Procedure. It is important that teachers support students in learning how this strategy works and why it is useful in taking notes. There are many important benefits of this strategy that can be shared with students:

- Note-Making provides a structure for turning notes into study tools by highlighting key words, summarizing, posing questions and making connections.

- Students have the opportunity to compare their notes with their neighbors and learn different strategies for note-making that can help with their own notes.

- Double Entry notes ensure that students think about the content of the lecture as they write, not simply write to get the information and facts into their notes.

- This strategy helps students catch up to the lecture if needed.

- Guided note-making can help to engage the class in discussions about taking notes, how to write notes in a structured way, and for students to discuss what works for them.

- Students can also discuss the value of the Guided Lecture experience, as well as any changes that would make the process work better for them.

It is important for teachers to foster class discussions in which students are coached in posing reflective, critical, and creative questions such as:

- What stands out for me?
- What questions would I ask about the ideas?
- How do I feel about this?
- Does this make sense?
- What does this text make me think of?
- How does this fit with what I already know?
- What might be added here? Omitted? Changed?
- Where can I apply these ideas?
- What do I agree/disagree with?
- What's not clear here?

Taking Reading Notes

The Guided Lecture Procedure, as on page 53, can also be applied to reading assignments, especially textbook reading. This process should be introduced in class, and practiced in a whole group setting to make sure that students know what is involved and what is expected of them. This process is especially helpful with textbooks and complex texts, but it can also be used with chapter books, short stories, poetry, and other texts that are a part of the curriculum.

The most effective way to introduce this process is by using a document camera that can project the teacher's notes as the students make their own. This allows the teacher's notes to act as a mentor text for the students in their own note-making, and provides a model for students. This can be a time consuming process at first, but becomes faster each time it is done. Once the teacher has introduced the activity and worked through it with the whole class, students can practice the activity in pairs, and then work independently while the teacher observes and helps students with the process. The steps for creating reading notes can be as follows:

1. Preview the text, then after examining it, make a one-page outline of key words or major ideas on the right side of a two-page spread. Turn headings of a text into questions.

2. Briefly read the text to summarize it, noting the important details under the key words and answering the questions as much as possible.

3. Reflective Critique: Critique the text by using questions like those in the Guided Lecture Method:

    - What stands out for me?
    - What questions would I ask about the ideas?
    - How do I feel about this?
    - Does this make sense?
    - What does this text make me think of?
    - How does this fit with what I already know?
    - What might be added here? Omitted? Changed?
    - Where can I apply these ideas?
    - What do I agree/disagree with?
    - What's not clear here?

4. Recite major ideas and supporting details without looking at the notes as much as possible.

5. Review the notes recite again on subsequent days.

6. Reflect on the text by going back to consider the significance of the content and the usefulness of the double entry notes and outline.

Studying for Exams

Many students have not mastered study skills by the time that they are even in high school, and benefit from direct instruction of these skills within the context of content area classrooms. There are many ways to study and methods that students can put into action to learn and practice in preparation for a test. Rote memorization is not helpful for long-term learning, and does not help students make sense of content or reflect on their learning. As students prepare for a summative assessment, they can review the notes that they created in response to their class and their reading, and also to reflect on how their learning is connected. Teachers should provide time for students to review their notes in the classroom, and coach them on further notating their lecture guides and reading notes. This can be done using a highlighter or different colored pen to underline and outline some of the most important areas of the notes or to create summaries, review cards and practice questions based on their notes. In addition to these methods, students can prepare and answer questions similar to those likely to appear on their exams. See the activity Create Your Own Test on page 59 for this activity. Teachers can share their thinking and provide students with examples of the kinds of essay and short answer questions and formats they might choose to use. Students working in small groups can then formulate their own questions and share them with the class in a question/answer format. This activity can replace formal review lectures in preparation for an exam or serve as an alternative for a mid-unit review.

These activities may seem to take valuable time from an already crowded curriculum. Research and experience has demonstrated, however, that few high school students, including the most advanced, learn best when studying independently. They expect to be spoon-fed the information that they need in order to succeed, and they often are. They are uncomfortable with uncertainty in their learning and often want to be assured that they have the right answer or are making the right connections. Unfortunately, even the most able students are likely continue with higher education without the skills needed to do the many demanding assignments they will face on their own. Struggling with learning is challenging, and many students become frustrated with the struggle. When that challenge can be first overcome with the support and assistance of teachers, students are likely to create new ways of dealing with those types of educational struggles and develop grit and resilience in pursuing their learning both in college and beyond.

A Final Word

By the time students leave high school they should be reflective, strategic, independent and interdependent learners. Achieving those objectives requires teachers to incorporate as much reading, writing and talking into their lessons as possible, and also to infuse metacognition and strategies to support such reflection. Learning is not passive, and students must become reflective learners—not just to the content they are learning but also to the ways in which they learn and the strengths and needs that they bring to the classroom. Using metacognition, students become strong lifelong learners and a willingness to look inwards to see how they learn best.

Chapter 10: Assessment For And Of Active Learning

The country is at a critical juncture in its effort to raise standards. The growing public reaction *against testing is fueled by excessive testing that is not aligned to curriculum, and the increasing pressure on teachers to "teach to the test" at the expense of real learning.*

Richard W. Riley

Assessing learning can take many different forms and serve a variety of purposes. Performance based literacy assessment can be an option for teachers in addition to summative assessments that support the classroom curriculum. This chapter offers an explanation and some examples of performance-based literacy evaluation for learning, consistent with The Five Reading, Writing and Talking Processes.

These assessments can include observations, documentation, portfolios, conferences, interviews, oral/written retellings and ways of determining students' Instructional, Independent and Frustration Reading Levels and Graphophonic Profiles, among others.

Peter Sacks, in *Standardized Minds*, documents in great detail what educators have said for many years: standardized tests often reward students' passive, superficial learning, drive instruction in undesirable directions, and thwart meaningful educational reform.

As Wellstone stated,

> *Making students accountable for test scores works well on a bumper sticker and it allows many politicians to look good by saying that they will not tolerate failure. But it represents a hollow promise. Far from improving education, high stakes testing (standardized testing as the single decision for important decisions) marks a major retreat from fairness, from accuracy, from quality and from equity... Studies indicate that public testing encourages teachers and administrators to focus instruction on test content, test format and test preparation.*

In the above citations, Sacks, Wellstone, Stiggins, and Meier propose a refocusing of educational practice and assessment to what students actually do in school rather than how they perform on standardized tests. Specifically, assessment should focus on active skills of learning, such as writing, speaking, and reading authentic texts, acting, drawing and investigating. According to Sacks, political motivation, rather than sound educational reasons, has propelled the overuse of standardized tests in schools, particularly in generating instructional practices.

Constructing Active Learning Assessments

Designing comprehensive assessment and accountability procedures is important in supporting the classroom learning and providing feedback in many areas, specifically in terms of student achievement, curriculum development and program design. Schools need to document and account for student learning and document the case that active student engagement and co-construction in the pursuit of excellence in individual classrooms and the school or district at large is the goal of education.

Evaluation should incorporate skills, strategies and content.

Language skills are acquired in activities of learning something, and that 'something' is the subject matter of English, social studies, science, math, and other content areas. Learning in these content areas depends on students using The Five Reading, Writing and Talking Processes and The Four Lenses of Learning.

Evaluation should put emphasis on assessment through observation.

Students' use of language is a complex, multi-faceted phenomenon. Teachers see learners in a variety of settings throughout the course of the day engaged in multiple activities. Much of what teachers want to know about students' learning cannot be derived from the results of assessments that reduce the complexity of student learning to written responses. Educators can observe, document and interpret a wide range of students' performance to construct a much deeper, and accurate, picture of student learning.

Evaluation should focus on student behaviors that relate to improvement.

The emphasis of assessment should be on information that can be translated into plans for instruction. Grades do not inform instruction as much as comments on students' reading interests, strengths and weaknesses of their writing samples, use of strategies in reading, and instructional and independent reading levels that come from informal reading inventories.

Using standardized tests and deconstructing test scores to evaluate students strengths and weaknesses for this purpose is unscientific and damaging, as there are serious issues with unreliability in relation to these sub-scores. Furthermore, those test results imply a diagnostic value that is not present when it comes to best practices teaching.

Evaluation should provide insights.

Students bring many perspectives to the school environment — differences that evolve from their diverse experiences. Instruction and assessment that are responsive to and respectful of the unique frame of reference that each learner brings can be more effective in establishing trends, accounting for changes and improvement and creating measures to help students who struggle. This type of assessment can effectively measure what students know, how they know it, and what significance it has in their school, home and community.

Evaluation should involve self-assessment and peer assessment.

An important part of becoming an independent learner is to reflect on one's own use of language. Students should have the opportunity to self-assess in a variety of ways, including their own content mastery, language skills, and writing ability. Furthermore, student collaboration can provide opportunities for peer coaching and assessment in a supportive, collaborative and cooperative way. This can come in the form of a peer review of writing, cooperative learning and assessment, creating and taking tests together, and developing strategies for this collaborative assessment. Through self-assessment, students become familiar with their own reading and writing skills and become more skilled at communicating with their peers in a way that drives the learning deeper.

Evaluation needs to be varied and differentiated.

Students and teachers are primarily concerned with assessment that provides insight into students' learning on a day-to-day basis. This comes from ongoing observations of how and what students learn in each subject. Additional types of assessment are more useful in addressing the needs and purposes of other constituencies: parents, administrators, school board members, and taxpayers. Parents may want to see samples of their children's work and commentary from teachers in addition to their grades. School board members and taxpayers want to see results of the performance of the group on tests that measure the student body, and administrators need to have access to all of the assessments, including those at a student, class, school and district level. Classroom or student grades and statistics without context or explanation can limit how these statistics are used, especially if they are not enhanced by anecdotal accounts from the teacher on of how students are learning, how well they are performing in class activities and assignments, and what content students are learning.

Procedures For Evaluation and Assessment

Active learning skills are often called "performance-based assessments". These incorporate products, performances, and process-focused assessments. Products include teacher or district constructed tests and quizzes, stories, poems, plays, research reports and portfolios. Performances include oral reports, enactment, dance and debates. Process-focused assessments include observing, documenting and conferencing.

The examples of assessments provided below incorporate performance–based assessments, including teacher observations and documentation, developing portfolios, oral and written retellings, Informal Reading Inventories, Graphophonic Profiles (for those still reading below a fourth grade instructional level), as well as teacher-made tests and exams.

Classroom Observation and Documentation

The Five Reading, Writing and Talking Processes emphasize the processing of ideas through extensive reading, writing, and speculative talking, as well as more collaborating and more choice of books topics and ways of responding, and there is much to observe, value, and evaluate. Teachers are continually evaluating students as they observe their classroom learning behavior, and know that teaching and evaluating are reciprocal processes, and that there are ways of enhancing these observations. Keeping anecdotal records of students or classroom events, teachers can remember and reflect on particular students' behaviors in the context of their interactions with their peers and with the expectations of the curriculum. Simply reflecting on a lesson in a lesson plan book or a by keeping an ongoing reflection in a document on a computer can help to make this easier for teachers to manage. Assessing of individual students is reflective of the relationship between the learner's activities and the learning environment in the classroom as well. Thus, if a student performs poorly on a test, it is important to reflect on that performance in relation to the performance of the rest of the class as well.

These and other methods of documenting observations make it possible to analyze and reflect on the learning in action. They also inform decisions about classroom management and curriculum, provide data for consultations with students and parents, and become the basis for reporting progress and problems. Extensive documentation might be limited to one or two students about whom the teacher is concerned.

Teachers can also enlist other teachers in the school, including Reading Specialists, Special Education teachers, Literacy Coaches and other teachers or administrators to observe and document the behavior of a student, a group, or an entire class. If the observations are made in response to a problematic situation in the classroom, the teachers can collaborate when solving these problems. This is best when teachers can discuss the area or student of focus in a pre-observation conference, which can then be followed by a visit (or visits) to the classroom to observe and document the problem identified by the teacher. This provides the context of ongoing learning events involving the entire ecology of the classroom. After the classroom visit, all teachers can collaborate on the observations and possible course of action.

Reading Portfolios

Reading portfolios can be excellent assessment tools for evaluating students during Transactions with Text and Extending Reading and Writing lessons. They should include samples of students' writing from assigned literary and expository texts or from self-selected books. More specifically they might include such pieces as

- Dialectical journals and learning logs

- A critical review of a story

- Notes on a textbook chapter

- Self-selected books read independently with writing about some aspect of selected books

- A written reflection on a key concept in the text

- A paragraph on "What stood out for me?" in response to an editorial or feature article

- A write up of a science experiment

- An advertisement to sell a book

- A retelling of a story

Grading some of these selections might be accomplished using a standardized system, either utilized just in the class or possibly adopted by a grade level or school. Rubrics can be especially helpful in evaluating consistently, and this tool takes time away from what can be a time-consuming process.

Writing Portfolios

Maintaining writing portfolios can be a good way to evaluate Composing Text and Extending Reading and Writing. These portfolios enable teachers and students to collect and evaluate writing periodically and cumulatively. Conferences with students and parents are more substantive when the students' writing portfolios are available for review.

Teachers also use student writing samples for common assignments or specially designed prompts to assess writing ability. In this case, teachers should make sure to show multiple samples of the completed assignments in order to illustrate the variety of student abilities and to highlight the genres and improvement over time.

Writing that calls for analysis, synthesis, interpretation and evaluation enables the learner to process information deeply. Therefore, analysis of a collection of a student's written work in every subject creates a solid basis for identifying instructional needs, for instructional decision making, for informing parents about their students' work, and for assigning final grades.

In every subject and class, students can keep dated written work in a portfolio, either as a hard copy or in a digital format. This collection can include academic journals, reports, essays and compositions, including notes and drafts of some writing as well. These portfolios can be graded periodically, with students selecting pieces they want to revise for the teacher to then grade.

Tests and Exams

Teachers give students many different kinds of quizzes, tests and exams that measure their knowledge of the subjects they teach. Here are some of the ways such evaluations can link language and learning:

- Most tests should include questions that require students to develop ideas in writing.

- Objective tests can sometimes call for a short paragraph allowing for explanation and elaboration of choices.

- More open book tests can be given, thus allowing for more thoughtful reflection.

- Students can work in teams to prepare tests and create collaborative answers.

- Students can be given a choice of which questions to answer on a test.

- Spelling, phonics and vocabulary tests should be contextualized rather than presented on lists.

- Tests calling for oral reading should allow for rehearsal and repeated readings.

- Time limits should be removed.

- Multiple-choice formats might be redesigned to allow for a broader range of responses.

A Final Word

Time is a precious commodity for teachers. They cannot afford to take time away for teaching, learning and assessing that is not productive. As we have seen in this chapter, though total standardized scores do provide reliable measures of learning for large groups that is useful to administrative and lay audiences, assessment for learning best informs teacher practice in the service of co-constructionist teaching and learning. Four general kinds of practices seem to be most productive for co-constructionist assessment for learning.

First, teachers can observe and document students' active skills: their thinking, listening, talking, reading, writing, enacting and investigating linguistic patterns. Second, teachers and students together can collect and reflect on samples of students' work. Teachers might compile this work in portfolios with a forewords written by the students that explains their rationale for including these items, and why they feel that they represent what and how they learned and what it means for their learning in the future. Third, teachers can use oral and written retellings to provide both a qualitatively rich learning experience and to use the product of this experience to assess students' writing abilities in terms of both content and Standard English usage. Fourth, teachers can determine regularly, through criterion-referenced assessments, the Reading Instructional and Independent Levels of all students and the Phonics Profiles of primary grade students, with the latter especially important for struggling readers. Finally, there are quizzes and exams developed by the teacher on current topics. These are among the kinds of assessment that are congruent with The Five Reading, Writing and Talking Processes and The Four Lenses of Learning.

Glossary of Terms

Accountability: This is the idea that teachers (or administrators) need to prove what they are doing and how well they are doing it. Accountability can be showing students' progress and their work. It can also be students' responsibility for completing their schoolwork.

Adaptive: If something is adaptive it can be changed to fit the situation. Adaptive teaching strategies often talk about ways to change teaching methods to work for all kinds of students.

Alignment: When ideas (in this case curriculum) are in an order that makes sense, and is matched to other ideas (for example, the elementary and secondary curriculum can be aligned to one another.)

Best practices: The best ways of doing things; a way of categorizing the best (most efficient) strategies that people use.

Building blocks: The idea of building blocks relates to the foundation or way of doing something. In this case, the building blocks are The Five Reading, Writing and Talking Processes.

Co-construction: We use "co" to mean together, therefore co-construction is people (policy makers, teachers, administrators, and students) working together to understand, explain, teach and make meaning.

Collaborative: When 2 or more people work together to help make something or understand something.

Disciplines: Areas of study

Fishbowl Activity: An activity where the teacher and small group of students show the rest of the class how to work together. The rest of the class watches and learns about what the teacher expects.

Imperative: Necessary and important. If something is imperative, it has to be done.

Interconnected: When things are connected to one another. Interconnected is similar to connected, but usually for more than 2 things.

Internalization: If you internalize something it becomes a part of you. For example, internalizing knowledge means you do not have to think about something; you just know it.

Intrapersonal: Intrapersonal is interaction between people and an understanding of the way people interact.

Meaning: In this text, the idea of "meaning" is used a lot. It can be similar to relevance, understanding, or significance. Meaning is something that is made or constructed by readers, teachers and students. Meaning is not just something that is waiting to be found. It is a thought process.

Measurable: Something can be measure; used in this book to talk mostly about tests and other assessments that people think can show exactly how much students have learned.

Metacognitive: Metacognitive is, basically, "thinking about thinking." It is knowledge and understanding the way that we think through things—being aware of what we're doing.

Paradigm: A paradigm is the common way of thinking, and the usual, traditional cause and effect or situation.

Phonemic: Phonemes are the smallest sounds that exist in the language. For example, the word "cat" has three phonemes.

Phonics: A system of teaching reading and writing by understanding and learning specific phonemes (sounds).

Scaffold: If a lesson is supported giving students help in completing the steps in the lesson. For example, when the teacher gives the students words to start their answers.

Seasoned Teacher: A teacher who is experienced and has been teaching for many years.

Social constructs: Social constructs are the parts of our society--for example cultural practices-- that have been created by interactions between people and throughout history.

Systematic: If something is systematic it is in all parts of something. For example, instead of teaching reading just in reading class, those skills are in every part of the curriculum.

Transacting: To transact with text means to interact with it; not just read but also make meaning, thinking about the writer's perspective, taking notes, and many other strategies.

Underpinnings: Ideas, concepts and theories that support and are the foundation (base) for this work.

References and Resources

Adams, M.J. (1990). Beginning To Read: Thinking And Learning About Print. Cambridge, MA: MIT Press.

Allington, R. W., & Walmsley, S. A. (1995) No Quick Fix: Rethinking Literacy Programs In America's Schools. New York: Teacher's College Press.

Anderson, R. C., Hiebert, E. H., Scott, J. A., & Wilkinson, I. A. G. (1985). Becoming A Nation Of Readers: The Report Of The Commission On Reading. Washington, DC: U. S. Department of Education.

Anderson, R., Hiebert, E. & Wilkinson I., (1984). Becoming A Nation Of Readers: The Report Of The Commission On Reading. Washington, DC: National Institute of Education.

Ashton-Warner, Silvia. (1963) Teacher. New York, NY: Simon & Schuster.

Atwell, Nancy. (1987) In the Middle: Writing, Reading, and Learning with Adolescents. Portsmouth, NH; Heinemann/Boynton/Cook.

Bakhtin, M.M. (1981). The Dialogic Imagination. Austin, TX: University of Texas Press.

Beach, R. (1985) Strategic teaching in literature. In Strategic Teaching And Learning: Cognitive Instruction In The Content Areas. Alexandria, VA ASCD.

Beck, I.L., & McKeown, M.G. (2001). Text Talk: Capturing The Benefits Of Read Aloud Experiences For Young Children. The Reading Teacher, 55, 10–20.

Beck, I. L., McKeown, M. G., & Kucan, L. (2008). Creating Robust Vocabulary: Frequently Asked Questions And Extended Examples. New York: Guilford Publications.

Beck, I. L., McKeown, M. G., & Kucan, L. (2013). Bringing Words To Life, Second Edition: Robust Vocabulary Instruction (2nd ed.). New York: Guilford Publications.

Bloome, D. (1985). Reading as a social process. Language Arts, 62(7).

Botel, M. (1978) A Pennsylvania Comprehensive Reading/Communication Arts Plan. Harrisburg, PA: The Department of Education of the Commonwealth of Pennsylvania.

Botel, M., Botel-Sheppard, B. K. & Renninger, A. B. (1994) Facilitating Change In The Schools. In Integrating Language Arts: Controversy to Consensus. New York: Allyn & Bacon.

Botel, M. Learning To Learn. In The Essentials Of Education, a document issued by 22 National professional education associations.

Botel, M., Ripley, P., & Barnes, L. (1992). A Case Study Of An Implementation Of The New Literacy Paradigm. In the British Journal of Reading Research.

Britton, J. (1970). Language And Learning. New York: Penguin.

Bruner, J. (1961). The Process Of Education. Cambridge, Massachusetts: Harvard University Press.

Bruner, J. (1973). On Knowing: Essays For The Left Hand. New York: Antheneum.

Bruner, J. (1983) In Search Of Mind. Harper and Row.

Bussis, A. M. & Chittenden, E. A. (1987, March). Research Currents: What The Reading Tests Neglect. Language Arts, National Council of Teachers of English.

Calkins, L (1986) The art of teaching writing. Portsmouth, NH: Heinemann.

Carleton, L., & Marzano, R. J. (2010). Vocabulary Games For The Classroom. United States: Marzano Research Laboratory.

Carini, P. F., & Himley, M. (Eds.). (2000). From Another Angle: Children's Strengths And School Standards: The Prospect Center's Descriptive Review Of The Child. New York: Teachers College Press.

Caswell, L. J., & Duke, N. K. (1998). Non-Narrative As A Catalyst For Literacy Development. Language Arts, 75, 108–117.

Cazden, C. B., Cordeiro, P., Giacobbe, M. E., Clay, M. E, & Hymes, D. (1992). Whole Language Plus: Essays On Literacy In The United States And New Zealand. New York: Teachers College Press.

Cazden, C. (1992). Whole Language Policy: Essays On Literacy In The United States And New Zealand. New York: Teachers College Press.

Chall, J. (1983). Learning To Read: The Great Debate. New York: McGraw-Hill.

Chomsky, C. (1971, March). Write First, Read Later. Childhood Education.

Chomsky, C. (May 1970). Reading, Writing, And Phonology. Harvard Educational Review, 40, 2.

Cochran-Smith, M., & Lytle, S. L. (1993). Inside/Outside: Teachers Research And Knowledge. New York: Teachers College Press.

Cole, N. S. (1988). A Realist's Appraisal Of The Prospects For Unifying Instruction And Assessment, Assessment in the Service of Learning, Invitational Conference Proceedings of the Educational Testing Service. Princeton, NJ: Educational Testing Service.

Coleman, D., & Pimental, S. (2012). Revised Publishers' Criteria For The Common Core State Standards In English Language Arts And Literacy, Grades 3–12. Washington, DC: Council of Chief State School Officers. Retrieved from http://groups.ascd.org/resource/documents/122463-PublishersCriteriaforLiteracyforGrades3-12.pdf

Collins, John J. (2012). Improving Student Performance Through Writing And Thinking Across The Curriculum. West Newbury, MA: Collins Education Associates.

Cunningham, A. E., & Stanovich, K. E. (2001). What Reading Does For The Mind. Journal of Direct Instruction, 1(2), 137–149.

Cunninghamm, J. W. (2001). The National Reading Panel Report. Reading Research Quarterly 36, 326-335.

Darling-Hammond, L. (1994). Performance-Based Assessment And Educational Equity, Harvard Educational Review, 64, (1), 5-30.

Darling-Hammond, L. (1994). National Standards And Assessment: Will They Improve Education? American Journal of Education. (pp. 479-510). University of Chicago

Davidson, J. L. (Eds.). (1988). Counterpoint And Beyond: A Response To Becoming A Nation Of Readers. Urbana, Illinois: National Council of Teachers of English.

Delpit, L. (1995). Other People's Children: Cultural Conflict In The Classroom. New York: The New Press.

Dillner, M. (2001). Using Media Flexibly To Compose And Communicate. *Reading Online, 5*(1). Available: http://www.readingonline.org/articles/art_index.asp?HREF=/articles/dillner/index.html

Dyson, A.H. (1987) The Value Of "Time Off Task" Young Children's Spontaneous Talk And Deliberate Text. Harvard Educational Review. 57 (4): 395-420

Edelsky, C. (1991). With Liberty And Justice For All: Rethinking The Social In Language And Education. Bristol, PA: The Falmer Press.

Ehri, L.C., Nunes, S.R., Willows, D.M., Schuster, B.V., Yaghoub-Zadeh, Z., Shanaham, T. (2001). Phonemic Awareness Instruction Helps Children Learn To Read: Evidence From The National Reading Panel's Meta- Analysis, Reading Research Quarterly, 36, 3, 250-287

Elbow, P. (1987) Embracing Contrasts: Explorations In Teaching And Learning. New York: Oxford University Press.

Elley, W.B., Schleicher, A., & Wagemaker, H. (1994). Introduction. In W.B. Elley (Ed.), The IEA study of reading literacy: Achievement and instruction in thirty-two school systems (pp. 1-33). Oxford, England: Pergamon.

Fader, D., Duggins, J., Finn, T., & McNeil, E. (1976). The New Hooked On Books. New York: Berkley Publishing Corporation.

Fisher, D., Frey, N., & Lapp, D. (2012). *Text Complexity: Raising Rigor In Reading.* Newark, DE: International Reading Association.

Freire, P. (1987). The Importance Of The Act Of Reading. In P. Freire & D. Macedo (Eds.), Literacy: Reading the word and the world (pp. 29-36). S. Hadley, MA: Bergin & Garvey.

Garan, E.M. (March 2001). Beyond The Smoke And Mirrors: A Critique Of The National Reading Panel Report On Phonics. Phi Delta Kappan (pp. 500-506).

Gardner, H. (1983). Frames Of Mind: The Theory Of Multiple Intelligences. New York: Basic Books.

Gee, J. P. (1996). Social Linguistics And Literacies: Ideology In Discourses (2nd ed.). Bristol, PA: Taylor & Francis.

Gewertz, C. (2012). Districts Gird For Added Use Of Nonfiction. *Education Week, 31*(12), pp. 1, 14.

Gibson, E. J. & Levin, H., (1975). The Psychology Of Reading. Cambridge, Massachusetts: MIT Press.

Gleitman, L. R. & Rozin, P., (1977). The Structure And Acquisition Of Reading I: Relations Between Orthographies And The Structure Of Language. In A. S. Reber & D. L. Scarborough (Eds.), Toward A Psychology Of Reading. Hillsdale, New Jersey: Erlbaum.

Goodlad, J (1984) A Place Called School. New York: McGraw-Hill.

Goodman, K (1986) What's Whole In Whole Language? Portsmouth, NH: Heinemann.

Graves, D. H. (1983). Writing: Teachers And Children At Work. Exeter, New Hampshire: Heinemann Educational Books.

Gunning, Thomas. (2012). Building Literacy In Secondary Content Area Classrooms. Boston, MA: Allyn & Bacon.

Heath, S.B. (1983). Ways With Words: Language, Life, And Work In Communities And Classrooms. Cambridge, UK: Cambridge University Press.

Hymes, D. (1974). Foundations Of Sociolinguistics: An Ethnographic Approach. Philadelphia, PA: University of Pennsylvania Press.

IRA/NTCE Joint Task Force on Assessment. (1994). Standards For The Assessment Of Reading And Writing. Newark, DE.

Jager Adams, M. (1990). Beginning To Read: Thinking And Learning About Print. Cambridge, Massachusetts: MIT Press.

Juel, C. & Minden-Cupp, C. (2000). Learning To Read Words: Linguistic Units And Instructional Strategies. Reading Research Quarterly, 35(4), 458-492

Kelley, M. J. and Clausen-Grace, N. (2010), Guiding Students Through Expository Text With Text Feature Walks. The Reading Teacher, 64: 191-195. doi: 10.1598/RT.64.3.4

Kinzer, C.K. (2003). The Importance Of Recognizing The Expanding Boundaries Of Literacy. Reading Online, 6(10). Available: http://www.readingonline.org/electronic/elec_index.asp?HREF=/electronic/kinzer

Knapp, M. S. (1995). Teaching For Meaning In High-Poverty Classrooms. New York: Teachers College Press.

Krashen, S. (1993). The Power Of Reading: Insights From The Research. Englewood, Colorado: Libraries Unlimited, Inc.

Krashen, S. (May 10, 2000). Reading Report: One Researcher's 'Errors And Omissions'. EDUCATION WEEK, Washington, D.C.

Krashen, S. (October 2001). More Smoke And Mirrors: A Critique Of The National Reading Panel Report On Fluency. Phi Delta Kappan (pp. 119-121).

Latest NAEP Sees Little Change In Past Eight Years. (June/July 2001). Reading Today. Newark, DE: International Reading Association.

Lytle, S. (1982) Exploring Comprehension Style: A Study Of Twelfth-Grade Readers: Transactions With Text. Ann Arbor, MI" University Microfilms International

Lytle, S. and Botel, M. (1989). The Pennsylvania Framework For Reading, Writing And Talking Across The Curriculum. Harrisburg, PA. The Pennsylvania Department of Education

Madaus, G. F. (1985). What Do Test Scores "Really" Mean In Educational Policy? In J. Beard & S. McNab (Eds.), Testing in the English language arts: Uses and abuses. Urbana, IL: National Council Of Teachers Of English. [Originally published by the Michigan Council of Teachers of English.

Marshall, J. C. (2002). Are They Really Reading? Expanding SSR In The Middle Grades. Stenhouse Publishers.

Marzano, R. J. (2000). A New Era Of School Reform: Going Where The Research Takes Us. Aurora, CO: McREL.

Marzano, R. J., & Pickering, D. J. (2005). Building Academic Vocabulary: Teacher's Manual. United States: Association for Supervision & Curriculum Development.

Marzano, R. J., & Simms, J. A. (2013). Vocabulary For The Common Core. United States: Marzano Research Laboratory.

Mason, J.M., Osborn, J.H., and Rosenshine, B.V. (1977). A Consideration Of Skills Hierarchy Approaches To The Teaching Of Reading. Technical Report No. 42. Champaign, IL: University of Illinois at Urbana-Champaign, Urbana, IL: National Council of Teachers of English.

Milliot, J. (2012, July 20). Industry Sales Pegged At $27.2 Billion. *Publishers Weekly.* Retrieved from: www.publishersweekly.com/pw/by-topic/industry-news/financial-reporting/article/53112-industry-sales-pegged-at-27-2-billion.html

Moffet, J. & Wagner, B. J. (1992). Student Centered Language Arts And Reading, K-13 (fourth edition). Portsmouth, NH: Boynton/Cook Publishers, Inc.

Moffet, J. & Wagner, B. J. (1993). What Works Is Play. Language Arts, 70, 32-36.

Murray, D. (1985). A writer teaches writing second edition. Boston, MA: Houghton-Mifflin.

National Council of Teacher of English. May 2004. A Call To Action: What We Know About Adolescent Literacy And Ways To Support Teachers In Meeting Students' Needs. November 2009. http://www.ncte.org/positions/statements/adolescentliteracy

National Institute of Child Health and Human Development (2000). Report Of The National Reading Panel. Teaching Children To Read: An Evidence-Based Assessment Of The Scientific Research Literature On Reading And Its Implications For Reading Instruction. (NIH Publication No. 00-4769). Washington, DC: U.S. Government Printing Office.

National Reading Council. (2000). National Reading Panel: Teaching Children To Read: An Evidence Based Assessment Of The Scientific Research Literature On Reading And Its Implications For Reading Instruction.[Online] Available: http://www.nationalreadingpanel.org.

National Governors Association Center for Best Practices & Council of Chief State School Officers. (2010).Common Core State Standards For English Language Arts And Literacy In History/Social Studies, Science, And Technical Subjects, Appendix A. Washington, DC: Authors. Retrieved from www.corestandards.org/assets/Appendix_A.pdf

Neil, M. & Medina, N. (1989). Standardized Testing: Harmful To Educational Health. Phi Delta Kappan, 70, 688-702.

Oakes, J. (1985). Keeping Track: How Schools Structure Inequality. New Haven: Yale University Press.

Porter, A., McMaken, J., Hwang, J., & Yang, R. (2011). Common Core Standards: The New U.S. Intended Curriculum. *Educational Researcher, 40,* 103–116.

Pressley, M., Billman, A. K., Perry, K.H., Feffitt, K. E. & Reynolds, J.M (eds.) Shaping Literacy Achievement: Research We Have, Research We Need , (pp246-249). New York: Guilford.

Preventing Reading Difficulties In Young Children. (1998). National Reading Council. Washington, DC: National Academy Press.

Principles and indicators for student assessment systems, (1995), National Reform On Assessment. Cambridge, MA: National Center for Fair & Open Testing (Fair Test).

Prospect Center Documentary Processes (1986), Bennington, VT: Prospect School.
   Putnam, L. (1982).   An Ethnographic Study Comparing A Traditional With An Experimental Approach To Reading Readiness Instruction. Urbana, Illinois: National Institute of Education.

Purves, A.C. & Elley, W.B. (1994). The Role Of The Home And Student Differences In Reading Performance, In W.B. Elley (Ed.),

The IEA study of reading literacy: Achievement and instruction in thirty-two school systems (pp. 89-121). Oxford, England: Pergamon.

Reis, S. M., Eckert, R. D., McCoach, D. B., Jacobs, J. K., & Coyne, M. (2008). Using Enrichment Reading Practices To Increase Reading, Fluency, Comprehension, And Attitudes. *Journal of Educational Research, 101*, 299–315.

Report of the National Early Literacy Panel (2008), Developing Early Literacy: A Scientific Synthesis Of Early Literacy Development And Implications For Intervention. National Institute for Literacy. Washington, D. C.

Rideout, V. J., Foehr, U. G., & Roberts, D. F. (2010). Generation M2: Media In The Lives Of 8- To 18-Year-Olds. Menlo Park, CA: Kaiser Family Foundation. Retrieved from www.kff.org/entmedia/mh012010pkg.cfm

Riley, R. W. (July 11, 2001). Investment Without Incentive, Bipartisan Support For Education Will Not Survive Under Funded Goals And Ideological Attacks. EDUCATION WEEK, Washington, D. C.

Rosenblatt, L. (1978). The Reader, The Text, The Poem. Carbondale, IL: Southern Illinois University Press.

Rosenblatt, L. (1985). The Transactional Theory Of The Literary Work: Implications For Research. In C. Cooper (Ed.), Researching response to literature and the teaching of literature. Norwood, NJ: Ablex.

Rozin, P. & Gleitman, L. R., (1977). The Structure And Acquisition Of Reading II: The Reading Process And The Acquisition Of The Alphabetic Principle. In A. S. Reber & D. L. Scarborough (Eds.), Toward a psychology of reading. Hillsdale, New Jersey: Erlbaum.

Sanacore, J., & Palumbo, A. (2009). Understanding The Fourth-Grade Slump: Our Point Of View. *The Educational Forum, 73*, 67–74.

Santos, F. (2011, April 24). A Trial Run For School Standards That Encourages Deeper Thought. *New York Times*. Retrieved from www.nytimes.com/2011/04/25/nyregion/100-new-york-schools-try-common-core-approach.html

Schon, D. (1983). The Reflective Practitioner. How Professionals Think In Action. New York: Basic Books.

Seaver, J. T. (1989). Making Sense Of Sentence-Making: Primary Grade Teachers' Assumptions Underlying Their Implementation Of An Inquiry Approach To Language Study. Unpublished Dissertation, University of Pennsylvania

Seaver, J. T. & Botel, M. (1991), Reading Writing Talking Across The Curriculum: A Handbook For Elementary And Middle Grade Teachers. Philadelphia, PA: Morton Botel Associates.

Shattuck, R. (1996). Forbidden Knowledge: From The Prometheus To Pornography. New York: Harcourt Brace & Company.

Sipe, L. (2000). The Construction Of Literacy Understanding By First And Second Graders In Oral Response To Picture Storybook Read-Alouds. Reading Research Quarterly, 35(2), 252-275

Smith, F. (1982). Understanding Reading (third edition). New York: Holt, Rinehart & Winston.

Smith, F. (1985). Reading Without Nonsense (second edition) New York: Teachers College Press.

Snow, C. E., Burns, M. S., & Griffin, P. (Eds.). (1998). Preventing Reading Difficulties In Young Children. Washington, DC: National Academy Press.

Stahl, S. A. Understanding Shifts In Reading And Its Instruction. In K.A.) Reading research at work. Foundations of effective practice (pp.45-75). New York. Guilford.

Stanovich, K. E. (1986). Matthew Effects In Reading: Some Consequences Of Individual Differences In The Acquisition Of Literacy. Reading Research Quarterly, 21(4), 360406.

Street, B. (1997). The Implications Of The New Literacy Studies For Literacy Education, English in Education, NATE, 31, 26-39.

Street, B. (1998). New Literacies In Theory And Practice: What Are The Implications For Language In Education? Linguistic and Education, 10, 1-24.

Street, B. (1995) Social Literacies. New York: Longman Group Limited.

Street, B. V. (1994). Struggles Over The Meaning(S) Of Literacy, In M. Hamilton & D. Barton & R. Ivanic (Eds.), Worlds Of Literacy (pp. 15-20). Clevedon: Multilingual Matters Ltd.

Street, B. V. (1999). The Meaning Of Literacy, In D. A. Wagner & R. L. Venezky & B. V. Street (Eds.), Literacy: An International Handbook (pp. 34-39). Boulder, CO: Westview Press.

Strickland, D. S. & Mandel Morrow, L. (Eds.). (2000). Beginning Reading And Writing. New York: Teachers College Press.

Supovitz, J. A. (November 5, 1997). From Multiple Choice To Multiple Choices, A Diverse Society Deserves A More Diverse System. EDUCATION WEEK, Washington, D.C.

Sutton-Smith, B. (Summer 1982). The Importance Of The Storytaker: An Investigation Of The Imaginative Life. The Urban Review, 8.

Taylor, D. (1998). Beginning To Read And The Spin Doctors Of Science: The Political Campaign To Change America's Mind About How Children Learn To Read. Urbana, Illinois: National Council of Teachers of English.

Taylor, B., Anderson, R.C., Au, K.H. & Raphael, T.E. (2000), Discretion In The Translation Of Research To Policy: A Case From Beginning Reading. Educational Researcher, 29, 16-26.

Teale, W. H. & Sulzby, E. (1986), Emergent Literacy: Writing And Reading. Norwood, NJ: Ablex.

Thorndike, R.L. (1973). Reading Comprehension Education In Fifteen Countries: An Empirical Study. New York: Wiley & Sons.

Tierney, R. (2000). Literacy Assessment Reform: Shifting Beliefs, Principled Possibilities, And Emerging Practices. In R. D. Robinson & M. C. McKenna & J. M. Wedman (Eds.), Issues And Trends In Literacy Education (pp. 115-135), Needham Heights, MA: Allyn & Bacon.

Trelease, J. (1979). The Read-Aloud Handbook. New York: Penguin Books.

Valencia, S. W. & Wixson, K.K. (2000) Policy-Oriented Research On Literacy Standards And Assessment. In M.L. Kamil, P.B. Mosenthal, P.D. Paterson, & R. Barr (Eds.), Handbook of Reading Research (pp. 909- 935). Mahwah, NJ: Erlbaum.

Vincent, D. & Street, B. (Eds.). (1993). Journal Of Research In Reading, 16(2): Special Edition: The New Literacy Studies. United Kingdom: Blackwell Publishers.

Vygotsky, L. S. (1962). Thought And Language. Cambridge, Massachusetts: MIT Press.

Vygotsky, L.S. (1978). Mind In Society: The Development Of Higher Psychological Processes.. Cambridge MA: Harvard University Press.

Wagemaker, H. (1993c). Summary-What The Study Tells Us. In H. Wagemaker (Ed.), Achievement In Reading Literacy: New Zealand Performance In A National And International Context (pp. 186-188). Wellington, New Zealand: Ministry of Education.

Walberg, H.J. & Tsai, S. (1984). Reading Achievement And Diminishing Returns To Time, Journal of Educational Psychology, 76, 442-451.

Wellstone, P.D. (Spring 2000). High Stakes Tests: A Harsh Agenda For America's Children. Fair Test Examiner.

Wiggins, G.P. (1992). Assessing Student Performance. San Francisco, CA: Jossey-Bass Publishers.

Writing Study Group of the NCTE Executive Committee. 2016. Professional Knowledge For The Teaching Of Writing. February 2016. Web. http://www.ncte.org/positions/statements/teaching-writing

Young, T. A., Moss, B., & Cornwell, L. (2007). The Classroom Library: A Place For Nonfiction, Nonfiction In Its Place. Reading Horizons, 48(1), 1–18.

Zygouris-Coe, V., Wiggins, M.B., & Smith, L.H. (2004). Engaging Students With Text: The 3-2-1 Strategy. The Reading Teacher, 58(4), 381–384.

Made in the USA
Middletown, DE
04 September 2022

73166104R00104